The Bright Side of African Life

ILLUSTRATED

BY

Hon. William H. Heard,

Minister Resident and Consul General of the United States to Liberia.

NEGRO UNIVERSITIES PRESS
NEW YORK

Originally published in 1898
by the A.M.E. Publishing House

Reprinted 1969 by
Negro Universities Press
A DIVISION OF GREENWOOD PUBLISHING CORP.
NEW YORK

SBN 8371-1817-4

HON. WILLIAM H. HEARD,
Ex-Minister to Liberia.

Preface.

Legation of the United States
Monrovia, Liberia,
Nov. 26, 1897.

My only reason for attempting to write this book is to clear a
sky that has always been cloudy, to bring to light many
things that are hidden, to tell the truth where many have
purposely dodged it, to make known the present and
future of a great country, as I see it. Shall I succeed?
I shall not color any facts, but lay them bare. I shall not
hide any lies, but cause the sun to shine upon them.

One only needs to lay bare facts and open to sunshine lies, to
make Liberia a prodigy. Why? How? and When? are
the questions that will come from those who have been
deprived of facts and to whom many lies have figured
as truths If I accomplish the above task, my highest am-
bition will be satisfied.

Yours for the advancement of Africa,

WILLIAM H. HEARD.

Introduction.

A BRIEF ACCOUNT OF LIBERIA, THE NEGRO REPUBLIC IN WEST AFRICA.

Liberia (liberty) is situated in West Africa, between 4°20' and 7° 20' North latitude. It was founded in 1822, as an asylum for the liberated and free blacks of North America, by the American Colonization Society in the United States—an organized expression of the Christian philanthropy of that country.

The first pieces of land bought from the natives were a small Island known as Providence Island, lying in the Messurado River, near its mouth, and the Cape "Messurado," on which Monrovia, the capital city, now stands.

Each succeeding year the Society sent out, in chartered vessels, people of color, as they were liberated by their masters in America, and who desired to return to their ancestral home. The increase of population made it necessary for the acquisition of more territory, hence the boundary of the colony was, from time to time, extended to six hundred miles of sea-coast and two hundred and fifty miles interiorwards. Since, however, the French took the Cavalla country, the sea-coast is reduced to 509 miles.

This home was not founded simply as a refuge from the bitter oppression of America, to which the Negro was subject, but that an opportunity might be given to them, on the soil of their fathers, to exercise their God-given powers in developing real manhood in every sense of the word; and, also, that they might teach their benighted brethren in Africa the way back to God.

The government of the colony was, for the most part, in the hands of white men, sent out from America by the Society, with the title of "Governors" until it was declared a Republic. Then and until now Negroes have ruled.

The aborigines being superstitious, and, further, demoralized by unprincipled Spaniards who, at that time, carried on a lucrative traffic on the West Coast, in that curse of curses—slavery, naturally resisted the colonists for a long time. They could not readily conceive that the settling of these people in their midst would be beneficial to them. Having no moral conception of the terrible misery they were entailing upon their people by selling them, they thought only of the seeming gain that was accruing to them by the traffic, and hence they were prepared to resist any and every agency that would have a tendency to undermine the nefarious barter.   The colonists, however, struggled on to maintain power and prestige, enduring untold hardships and sufferings, the contingencies of war. poverty, and inexperience, until they were masters of the situation.   The result of their sweat, blood, tears and prayers is the Republic of Liberia, the only free and independent home that the Negro can call his own in all Africa.

This Republic was founded in 1847, after the colony had existed twenty-five years.   The Society withdrew its supervision and left the people of the commonwealth to their own government, and on the 26th day of July, of the year named, they declared themselves a free and independent nation.   Since the declaration of independence, the Republic has been recognized by and is in treaty stipulations with, all the Powers of Europe and the United States of America. England was the first to extend the hand of fellowship to Liberia as a nation.

The Republic is modeled after that of the United States of America, having three co-ordinate branches of government, viz: Executive, Legislative and Judicial.   The Executive is composed of the President and his Cabinet; the Legislative, of a Senate and House of Representatives; the Judiciary, of the Supreme and Inferior Courts.

The Republic is divided into four counties, namely, Montserrado, Grand Bassa, Sinoe, and Maryland.   And the counties are divided into towns and villages   There are many denominations in Liberia endeavoring to do Christian work on Apostolic lines.   They build their own churches and the ministers preach the gospel and support themselves with their own hands.   One denomination alone has founded thirty-one churches and three schools for the training of the youths of the country; others are doing more or less according to their ability.   The government partially supports about forty-six schools that are open to all without charge.

· Liberia is struggling to maintain its existence and to hold up the light of Christianity to its own people through poverty and inexperience.   For forty-nine years it has existed as a nation, and during that time thousands of the aborigines have been brought under the influence of Christianity and civilization, and to-day they are clothed and in their right minds and enjoying Christianity.

It is my purpose to show the present and future grandeur of this black Republic, its agricultural wealth, its mercantile enterprise and political, educational and religious progress.

LIBERIA.

In the settlement of Liberia, as in the case of all new countries over untried seas, surrounded by strangers and enemies, many hardships were experienced before a footing was obtained.

The first people who attempted to settle Liberia left New York the 6th day of February, 1822, but it was fully two years before they reached Cape Montserrada where Monrovia now stands. Freetown, Sierra Leone, was first reached, but not desiring to be entangled with other governmen s, the colony, after wandering around Sierra Leone at Fourali Bay, moved southward to Sherboro. In January, 1822, they reached Perseverance Island in the mouth of the Montserrado River, and purchased that Island and Cape Montserrado from King Peter, a native ruler. The agreement was signed by Robert F. Stockton and Dr. Eli Ayres, representing the Colonization Society, and five of the original eighty persons who left New York February 6, 1822.

This cape and island purchased the foundation of the Republic of Liberia was laid; yet this was not the selection of the Board of Managers of the Colonization Society, for they preferred Axim, but Commodore Stockton decided this to be a more desirable spot. The money was paid and the asylum for the oppressed secured. After this, many purchases were made, until the Republic reached from the Manna River on the north to the Cavalla River on the south, and interiorward to the Mandingo French possessions, covering an area of six hundred miles on the coast and two hundred and fifty miles into the interior, 50,000 square miles, sufficient territory to settle all the Negroes in America. The climate is varied and the soil productive, minerals abound and the resources are unlimited.

CAPE MOUNT.

Cape Mount is the most northern point. It is a mountain lying on the sea; yet, while mountainous, it is as fertile as any part of Western Africa. I have seen upon the highest point, coffee growing and gardens and farms as prolific as any on the St. Paul, Messurado or June rivers.

Farming is carried on extensively on this mountain, fruits are grown, vegetables are produced in abundance; more than can be consumed is produced yearly. The land has qualities that indicate the exist ence of iron, silver and gold in abundance. ·It reminds one very much of the city of Freetown – that is Robertsport, the town of Cape Mount, does. The farmers are emigrants from America and they are thrifty and prosperous. Among the farmers are Messrs. Hall,White and Askie.   Mr. White is from South Carolina and Mr. Askie is from North Carolina.

The Huffs are among the leading men of Cape Mount.

Hon. Jacob Huff was born in Georgia about fifty-two years ago, and came to Cape Mount in 1857. He has done more to build up this part of Liberia than any man whom I have the honor to know. He served as a private in the Pedee war at Cape Palmas. He rose from the office of constable to that of superintendent of Robertsport President Warner commissioned him constable in 1862, and seeing his ability, elevated him to Second Lieutenant in the army. He was com- missioned deputy sheriff by President Roye, but President Johnson discerning his efficiency as an officer, promoted him from deputy sher- iff to superintendent, or Governor, of Cape Mount. President Cheese- man renewed his commission, but as honesty is a quality that com- mends men, in 1896, President Cheeseman commissioned him Treas urer for Robertsport.

Hon. Mr. Huff married Miss Jones in 1864, and this happy union has resulted in nine children, who, like their parents, are making their mark in Liberia.

Hon. Robert H. Marshall, at Cape Mount, is the leading attorney. He has also a political record that makes him known throughout Li- beria, having represented Montserrado county in the lower house of the National legislature. He is an educated, progressive young man.

I cannot leave this part of the country which is so productive of palm oil, pysava, and palm kernels, without mentioning Mr. R. J. B. Watson. He is the leading merchant at this point, and is known by the natives far and near. He speaks Vey as well as the natives. He is a merchant king, and has done much to make Cape Mount a market that is equal to any in Liberia, except Monrovia and Grand Bassa.   Mr. Watson married the sister of the late General R. A. Sherman, and she has since been the power behind the throne.

Mr. WILLIAM H. ADAMS.
Philanthropic Farmer, Royesville, Liberia.

Mr. Robert H Gordon is a local attorney of note. He is one of those who has sustained his reputation as a patriotic citizen in peace and war, for here a native war was waged for ten years, and Mr. Gordon, with other good citizens, assisted by President Cheeseman, settled, once for all, this tribal rebellion. The educational interests of the youth are not neglected at this point The Episcopal Church has a flourishing school which is well manned.

Leaving Cape Mount, we proceed southward for twenty-five miles before reaching a settlement of civilized Liberio Americans.

ROYESVILLE.

The name of our next settlement is Royesville—named by President Roye. Do not understand me to say that the whole of the twenty-five miles is a waste. No; natives who make that country rich are settled every eight or ten miles; these cultivate rice, gather palm oil pysava and palm nuts. But Royesville is a new settlement; the land, which is very rich, grows coffee and sugar-cane, besides all the vegetables and fruits known to this Republic

Mr. William H. Adams is the prince of all this country He is the farmer, the merchant and the leader in church and state. Mr. Adams came from Charleston, S. C, in the "Azor" in 1878 ; since his arrival he has proven what can be done by push and energy. He is the leading farmer in all this country; his mercantile operations are extensive. He has a limited education, but ability to make and husband his resources; he has not forgotten Him in whom all must trust for success, so he employs his time in the Sunday School; and is the leading member of the A. M.E. Church; though 55 years of age, one would suppose him less than 45 The beautiful church building at Royesville is a monument to the sacrifice and energy of Mr Wm. H Adams. His name will never die in Royesville.

BREWERSVILLE.

The above settlement is one of the most populous in the Republic. The settlers are mostly from North Carolina, Virginia and Georgia.

The land is highly fertile and coffee is the main product; some of the best timber is back of this settlement on the Po River. The St. Paul River touches Brewersville on the South, and here is a dense mango swamp which makes it unhealthy to the "new comer." The minerals are copper and silver, while iron also abounds on the south border.

Some of the leading men of Montserrada County live in this settlement, one of whom Judge Parsons, who, for many years was Chief Justice of the Republic of Liberia, but who retired on account of blindness and age, is one of the most profound jurists that ever graced the Supreme Bench; though blind and retired, being at the advanced age of 78 years, he is sought as an authority in any and all difficult cases.

Hon. J. W. Parker, a member of the lower house of the General Assembly, also resides here in ease and comfort. He is a merchant, a farmer and a legislator; a young man of 40, who came from Georgia and settled here less than twenty years ago.

Hon. P. F Flowers, also a Georgian, resides here and is engaged in farming and mercantile pursuits; he came from Hawkinsville, Ga., less than twenty years ago, but now he lives in splendor. His farm is one of the most flourishing in the settlement. He is on the bright side of 45 years.

Captain H. C. Phelps, one of the leading military men of this township, came here from North Carolina He has one of the best companies of the militia of the Republic, and is also engaged as a merchant, and lives like a prince. It was my pleasure to spend a few days in his home, and I speak from experience. While burning with fever and agonized with pain, my every want was met. and such care given me as does not come to a stranger often in any country.

But the religious side of life is not neglected at Brewersville Here Rev. A. Cartwright, the superintendent of the A. M. E Z Church, resides. While superintending the Lord's vineyard, he does not neglect his own, for he has a splendid farm.

Rev. J O Hayes. also from South Carolina, is pastor of the Baptist Church, and principal of the public school. He is one of the most progressive man of his denomination in this country.

The Presbyterian Church has a good building and some very substantial members, but services are held irregularly for the want of a pastor

The African Methodist Episcopal Church was the last to enter this field, yet it has for its pastor at this writing, the Rev. C. Max Manning, A. M., Secretary of the United States Legation. Rev. J. R.

Gedda served this church, but antedating him was Rev. S. F. Flegler, of South Carolina.   Rev. A. L. Ridgel acted as pastor in 1895,
while filling the office of presiding elder.

WILLIAM BENJAMIN GAUNT,
Merchant at Brewersville. Liberia.

Mr. W. B. Gaunt is a leading merchant of Brewersville, and not to
give a short sketch of him would be to picture very faintly the progressive forces in this part of Liberia.

He was born in Mississippi, U. S., March, 1851, of slave parents,
and did not receive the boon of freedom until after Lee surrendered
to Grant in 1865.

Mr. Gaunt is a son of the soil, though engaged in other pursuits
as well, being also school-master and merchant.   His education was
obtained by his own efforts.   After teaching many years in his native
State, he married and then emigrated to Liberia, where he also engaged in teaching for several years.   Now he is one of the leading
merchants of Brewersville.   He goes to England and spends months
for health and recreation.

Judge Parsons, formerly of Charleston, South Carolina, one of the leading jurists of the Republic, resides at Brewersville, but he has retired, being aged and blind.   For many years he was Chief Justice of Liberia.

Hon. J. W. Parker, a member of the Legislature, also resides here, and as a merchant and farmer, is recognized as one of the foremost young men of Montserrado county.   We would be pleased to present his face which is so expressive of energy and pluck.

VIRGINIA.

This is a settlement four miles from Brewersville and on the banks of Stockton creek, about five miles from the city of Monrovia.   It is a farming settlement.   Mr. Sanders Washington, one of the most progressive men in Liberia, lives here.   He is active in the educational work, and a valuable member of the Baptist Church.   His home is graced by three grown up daughters, and it is a thing of beauty. These daughters are said to be the best dressed ladies in the Republic, but his extensive coffee farm upholds his luxury and cultivated tastes.

Rev. A. W. Watson has a farm at Virginia, and resides there.   He is also a progressive man and his family belong to the A. M. E. Church.   Miss Clarissa, his only daughter, is a most interesting and amiable lady of excellent influence

Ricks Institute, of which we shall speak later is not far from this landing.   Virginia is the landing for Brewersville.

CALDWELL.

This settlement and village is but a landing for farmers who have some of the best coffee farms on the St. Paul River.   The growers of coffee here are Messrs. Gibson, Yates and Ricks.

CLAYASHLAND.

This town,* as Arthington, has leading merchants, farmers and politicians.   Senator A B. King, the man who has done most to make Liberia known to the outside world, resides here.   He was the most prominent Liberian at the Chicago World's Exposition.

Senator King came to Liberia from Augusta, Ga., U.S.A., where he was born some forty years ago.

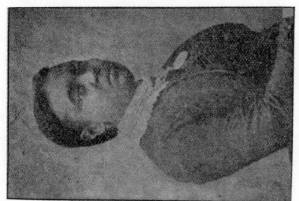

Mrs. A. B. KING,
Teacher at Clayashland,

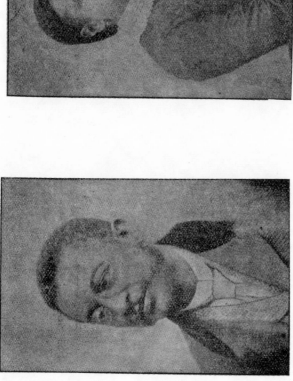

Hon. A. B. KING,
President Pro tempore of Liberia Senate.

He was quite a boy when he came to Africa, and a very poor boy, too. But knowing what there is in store for those who labor and sacrifice, he began to labor, though he had little to sacrifice. Knowledge being power, he obtained this and is now among the best educated men in Liberia; he loved knowledge and taught school himself for several years. One of the prettiest residences on the St. Paul River is that of Senator A. B. King at Clayashland; his farm is a model; he leads in politics in the Republic, and will, some day in the near future, reach the highest office, if he does not keep his head too warm—he only needs a cool head. As a mason, he is second in the Republic, being Deputy Grand Master. We present his face which speaks volumes. But in this case, as in many others, there is a power behind the throne, and to conceal that power is to conceal more than half of the truth. Such is Mrs. Florence King, the wife of Senator A. B. King, who is one of the leading teachers on the St. Paul River; she is companionable, intelligent, industrious and a lover of race and country. Liberia would not be what it is if it were not for many such women as Mrs. Florence King.

His Excellency, William David Coleman, one of the Republic's most successful farmers and merchants, resides at this point. His residence is the model for Liberia; every improvement that can be obtained, he has in his house. He is a wealthy man; he has been in politics for many years and has been elected Vice-President for three successive terms, and when President J. J. Cheeseman died, November 12, 1896, President Coleman succeeded him. He has not the education nor the originating faculty of the late President, but is a man of much common sense and is very economical in his habits; the very man for the Republic in this time of struggling to survive the billows of debt.

His countenance is expressive of determination, of honesty, and of faithfulness, all of which a man to be at the head of this nation needs. He does not drive men from him, his very face invites to better acquaintance. President Coleman is a Whig in politics and has received the nomination of his party, which is equivalent to election. We have faith in his future and Liberia's growth under him.

One of the leading men of Clayashland who deserves mention is John H. Ricks, who was born in Portsmouth, Va., January 4, 1846, and came to Liberia in 1853; his mother died the same year, therefore his education was blighted, but he was determined that his children should be educated and prepared for life's battle; and this has been fully carried out by him.   The father died in 1859, so John H. Ricks had to go out and live with others, receiving only $2.00 per month for his services.   He was converted in 1869, and connected himself with the A. M. E. Church.   Now he has his own farm.   He married in 1870; but his wife dying in 1874, he married again in 1876.

President WILLIAM D. COLEMAN,
Of Liberia.

The second wife was an emigrant from Columbus, Mississippi.   He began the cultivation of coffee—at first he had but fifty acres—now he has one of the most extensive farms in Liberia, 460 acres.   He has held the position of Tax Collector and Justice of the Peace, and is Manager of Rick's Institute, the leading school in Montserrado County.   As a military man, he served as Lieutenant and Captain. Liberia would not be what it is without John H. Ricks.   He has travelled in Spain, France and England.

Hon. J. H. RICKS,
A successful farmer of Clayashland, Liberia.

AUNT MARTHA RICKS,
Of Clayashland who has visited and dined with the Queen of England.

Mrs. Martha Ricks, or Aunt Martha as she is called by everybody, is of all the Rickses the most ancient and honorable, though in this settlement there are many wealthy and influential members of this family. She is noted for having visited the Queen of England and dined as her guest. Aunt Martha presented Queen Victoria with a quilt made by her own hands, the material of which cost $25.00; she makes no pretentions to book learning, yet she is a society lady. She is very religious, attending every convention, conference, quarterly meeting, and participating in the religious services; she is a Baptist by faith, yet no denomination is too humble for her to bow with in the celebration of the Lord's supper. She is demonstrative in her worship, but genuine religion is hers, and she enjoys "that peace which passeth all understanding." Though she has passed her three score and ten, she is still active and vigorous.

LOUISIANA.

In this settlement lives Major DeCorsey, one of the wealthiest men in Liberia. He is seventy-four years of age, and came to Liberia from Pennsylvania more than fifty years ago. He has engaged in farming on the improved style and has all the different kinds of fruit that grow in the tropical climate and all the vegetables that can be grown in this soil. His farm is as clean as the yard of the best kept house; his coffee farm is extensive, and $4,000 and $5,000 per annum is not extra for him to pocket at the sale of his coffee crop. The old gentleman does not take on any of the modern habits, and therefore we found it impossible to get a picture of such a valuable citizen; he has plenty of money and lives at ease. He is of medium size and height, very little education, but plenty of common-sense.

Senator R. H. Jackson lives in this settlement. He is a merchant, farmer and politician. His store at Louisiana is the leading business house in the community. Senator Jackson is a very progressive citizen and represents Montserrado County with honor to himself and country. He is yet a young man, and there remains promotion for him.

Beverly Yates Payne, a young man not yet forty, also lives in this settlement Col. Payne is a military man, and a leading politician. He is the Vice-Consul of the United States Legation, and is a most efficient officer, having filled this position for years. He has been the main officer here, receiving $4,000 per annum, which he has invested in coffee and used in building a mansion. In five years this will be one of the leading farms in Montserrado County. It will be the bank from which Col. Payne may draw continually in old age. There is not a citizen in Monrovia more winning than Beverly Y. Payne. We give you the picture of Col. Payne and the 5th Regiment.

One of the leading farms in this settlement is the property of the Sharpe estate. Jesse Sharpe was educated at Biddle University, North Carolina; married in Charlotte, N. C ; his wife is fast becoming a Liberian and Mr. Sharpe one of the foremost citizens of the community. He is quite young. but in the wearing of his hair he resembles the late Hon. Fred. Douglass of the United States.

MILLSBURG.

is a commercial centre. Here Rev. Clement Irons, who was one of the emigrants on the famous steamship Azor, lives and runs the steamboat Sarah Ann, which he built. This is the head of navigation on the St. Paul River. Rev. Clement Irons is quite an aged, white-haired father. He has spent more than twenty years in building up the A. M. E. Church, and by his labor the connection has churches in nearly every important town in Montserrado County, and several in Bassa County.

We would be pleased to give you a picture of the first steamboat that plies the Liberian waters, and then the old South Carolinian who invented and constructed this craft is a curiosity, indeed. His picture is worth the price of the book.

Herman Jager, a German, has a steamboat on the St. Paul, but it was built in Germany. Dennis Brothers, leading Liberian merchants, have managed to put a steamboat on the St. Paul, but it was constructed in England. The "Sarah Ann" constructed by a citizen of Liberia, is the pride of the people.

Hill and Moore, the leading merchants of Arthington, have a store at Millsburg.

Mr. George Wordsworth, of South Carolina is one of the farmers of this settlement. He is quite a unique character and quietly lives here in ease and comfort.

But a few miles from Millsburg is Muhlenburg, a Lutheran mission,

FIFTH LIBERIAN REGIMENT,
Commanded by Col. B. Y. Payne.

under the management of Mr. D. A. Day, who has resided at this point for twenty two years.   This is a beautiful location and none can visit it without admiring the push and energy put forth to make the surroundings what they are.

The raw native is taken from the bush, put into this school, educated and made a useful citizen of the Republic. The coffee farm on which they are taught the art of farming is one of the best cultivated in the Republic.   More than forty thousand pounds are gathered annually from this mission farm.   It is a mission self-supporting in the true sense of that word.   Until now, boys and girls have been educated together, but now, across the St. Paul River, in Harrisburg, the girls are to be educated separately, and taught civilization and handicraft also.   Dr. Day is the idol of many communities for miles around, though a white man.

ARTHINGTON.

In our descriptive travel we have reached Arthington, a settlement the most advanced in all the Republic of Liberia.   It was settled some seventeen years ago by people who migrated chiefly from South Carolina.   While they did not bring a cent of money, many of them brought manhood and pluck.

James De Lyon came among these.   He was a wild boy, and tried for years the life of a seaman; but finding as the years passed he was not one cent in advance of the previous year, he concluded to try coffee and ginger, planting more than one hundred acres: to-day he is classed among the progressive farmers of Liberia.   Mr. De Lyon is a young man, not yet having reached the meridian of life.   He has not had the advantages of an education, but by economy he has accumulated much and is now daily gathering about him this world's goods.   Mr. De Lyon is a radical African Methodist, believing it is the church for Liberia   He has done much to build up this branch of the Methodist faith.   He is a steward, trustee and leader of the local church at Arthington, and a member of many of the conference boards.

Another very active young man is James Haggard.   He is a young man, only a boy a few years since.   He has extensive property indeed, and is successful.   He is a leading member of the Methodist Church and has done all he could to aid in its success.

The name of Hill and Moore is a synonym for all that is progressive in Arthington and in Liberia.   Mr. Wallace F. Moore, the leading
business man in the firm, was born in South Carolina, York County,
in 1868.   His parents, Rev. June Moore and Adeline Moore, immi-
grated to Liberia in 1871, bringing Samuel, James and Wallace.   Rev.
June Moore is a Baptist preacher and believed that God desired him
to return to his fatherland to educate and rear his children.

WALLACE F. MOORE, ESQ.
Of the firm of Hill and Môore.

Wallace F. Moore was taught by his father at an early age—yet he
did not have a large stock to put out to his son—but Wallace was sent
to school to E. S. Morris and then to Rev. R. B. Richardson, D.D.
But his eyes failing, he was sent to the United States for treatment.
On returning, he was placed at Rick's Institute, the leading Baptist
school in Liberia.   During all this time the Moores were very poor
and could not afford to have a large boy at school all the while, so
Wallace went at intervals.   Like his father, however, he had ability,
and an opportunity was all he needed.   In 1890, he entered the

store at Monrovia, and thus finished his education in the practical s^hool of business.   He married Miss Hoggard in 1890, and is the happy father of two children and husband of an affectionate wife.   He is a leading member of the Baptist church.

He is superintendent of the Sabbath school.   He is also secretary of the Baptist Association, corresponding secretary and financial agent of the Baptist churches of the Association.   The firm of Hill and Moore, of which Wallace F. Moore is the leading business man, does more than one hundred thousand dollars worth of business annually.

Prof O. F Cook is a white man from New York, or Boston.   He is president of the Liberia College and agent for the Colonization Society; he has a large farm in this settlement at Mount Coffee.   I am told domestic slavery exists here, as it does on many farms owned and controlled by Afro Americans who were once slaves themselves, and that inhumanity plays its part with whip and driver.

Prof. Cook came to Liberia with the idea that the white man must rule under any and all circumstances, and that his agency for the Colonization Society and presidency of the Liberia College made him President of Liberia and manager of the United States Legation. Prof Cook is a learned man.   He spends about three months in Liberia looking a'ter the college and farm.   The other nine months the overseer controls the farm and slaves while the college is managed by a single professor.

The Colonization Society has missed its high and holy calling, and is now the seeker after gold and the enricher of an individual who has no interest in Liberia, only as it affords him comfort and puts dollars into his pocket.   Even the color line, I am told, has been tightly drawn by this learned professor.

CAREYSBURG

is one of the oldest and most homelike settlements in Montserrado. It is named for Rev. Lot Carey, one of the first settlers who came to Liberia.   The land is fertile and high and healthy.   Much coal could be obtained in the streets of Careysburg, but it is situated twenty miles from the Saint Paul River, and therefore, to reach it one must travel fully twenty miles on foot, or in a hammock, after leaving the waterway.   Copper could also be obtained in this settlement in large quantities

Some of the largest coffee farms in Liberia are at Careysburg. The Ureys have no end to their farms. Daniel Urey was one of the wealthiest farmers in Liberia. Dying, he left his children in good circumstances. He was unpretentious, yet he was a successful farmer.

Rev. R. M. J. Deputie, a Presbyterian minister who came to Liberia from Pennsylvania, has taught school and preached here for many years, thus making its school facilities second to none in the Republic. Rev. Deputie is also engaged in farming and is among those who successfully engaged in trying to build up this Negro Republic.

Rev. J. J Cuthbert, of the Baptist Church, lives in this settlement, and he is also engaged in building up the Republic, educationally, religiously and financially.

Hon Jerry C. Johnson member of the lower house of the Legislature, lives here and he also is among the successful farmers

Mr. Johnson was born in New Berne, North Carolina. July, 1856. He was brought to Liberia at the early age of two years, yet on account of the inhuman system of slavery that existed in the United States, the mother of Mr Johnson came to Liberia as a widow, as they were slaves and her husband did not happen to be the property of the same man she did—Colonel Wiley Nelson, who liberated her and four children, and they were sent to Liberia in 1858. They were situated at Careysburg, that is, their land was parcelled out in this settlement. The mother of Hon. Mr. Johnson was a woman who, after coming to a free country, desired to get all she could out of it for herself and children, so she sent them to school that they might obtain that which would fit them for future usefulness.

Rev. R. B. Richardson, D.D., one of the leading educators of Liberia, was teaching in the settlement of Liberia, and here for two years and six months Mr Johnson attended his school. But in 1875 the war at Cape Palmas called for all young men, and Mr. Johnson, being patriotic, left school and enlisted and was soon at the seat of war fighting his country's battles; but when the rebellion was crushed, he returned home and re-entered school. But as school closed he was forced to give up any further attempt to attend school, but became a teacher himself and taught ten years. He was then elected clerk of the court at Careysburg. He is not only busily engaged in the work of the State, but is a deacon and trustee in the Baptist Church,

Hon. J. C. JOHNSON,
Speaker of the House of Liberia.

Ex-PRESIDENT ROYE,
One of Liberia's wealthiest citizens.

superintendent of the Sunday school and treasurer of the church. He rose step by step and became assistant clerk of the Court of Quarter Sessions, then Deputy Sheriff, then clerk of the House of Representatives, and, in 1891, was elected a member of the House of Representatives, and Speaker of that body in 1895, which position he now fills with honor. Mr. Johnson married Miss Mary J. Kennedy in 1882. They are now a happy family and this lady presides over his city residence and commands at his farm, for Mr. Johnson is one of the leading coffee farmers of Careysburg.

REV. T. W. HAGAN, P.E.
Presiding Elder of the Monrovia District of the M. E. Church.

Rev. William T. Hagan, son of John and Sarah J., was born near Fayetteville, North Carolina, United States of America, October 10, 1843, of free parents, and lived in North Carolina until 1852; at which time John Hagan emigrated to Liberia with his family. On reaching Liberia in January, 1853, he settled at Millsburg on the St. Paul River. This was the extreme limit of any settlement at that time, but now many fine coffee farms are miles beyond, and the Muhlenburg Mission has been planted, one of the finest in the Republic.

Careysburg, his present home, was in the wilds at that time. Of the five children, three died before they were acclimated, many of the relatives died; his mother did not survive long. Within three years the family had well nigh died out, only five remained. He and his sister live now at Careysburg: She has two boys.

William was converted in a Methodist revival in 1856. He went with his father, in 1858, to assist in settling Careysburg. There being no church at Careysburg, he did not join the church until 1864. Rev. Daniel Ware came out, and under his ministry Mr. Hagan joined the M. E. Church.

He was soon appointed a steward and superintendent of the Sunday School, was licensed to exhort in 1869, licensed to preach in 1871, sent as a supply in 1872, and remained in this position until 1874, when he was received on trial in the conference. He preached and taught school for three consecutive years and was ordained Deacon by Bishop Haven in 1876. He was elected an Elder after a successful examination in 1879; but Bishop J. W. Roberts, the missionary, having died, and there being no Bishop in Africa, he was not ordained until 1885, then by Bishop William Taylor. The same year he was appointed Presiding Elder of the St. Paul River District. He presided over this district eleven years. He served one year at Careysburg, one year at Bensonville, three years at Millsburg and one year at Monrovia. In 1892, he was elected delegate to the General Conference of the M. E. Church. He was appointed Presiding Elder of the Monrovia District in 1896, and elected reserve delegate to the General Conference. Rev. J. H. Deputie, the regular delegate, having died, Mr. Hagan visited the General Conference of the great M. E. Church for the second time. He was a very successful pastor, and has few equals as a Presiding Elder. He is a lover of education, and does much in seeing that his brethren are supplied with books.

He has served his country in civil and military ways. He was captain of the militia and Mountain Regulars, and led in the wars of 1871 and 1875. He served as Justice of the Peace, Clerk of the Probate Court, Superintendent of Careysburg District two terms, Native African Commissioner and government surveyor, giving general satisfaction in each position. He was a candidate for the Senate in 1895, but was defeated by Senator A. B. King, a Whig. He married Miss Anna E. Richardson in 1871, and they have one daughter as the result of this union. Mrs. D. E. Howard, of Monrovia, is this daughter. His father lived until 1890. He left four sons and a second wife. Rev. Hagan is among the large coffee growers at Careysburg, and this is one of the largest coffee growing settlements in the Republic. The influence of such men as Rev. William T. Hagan has made it so.

JOHNSONVILLE.

This settlement is occupied mostly by new comers and has not yet been fully developed. Here many Kroomen have drawn land and have farms, but Kroomen do not make successful farmers; they are water animals.

Rev. H. W. White, of the A. M. E. Church, is one of the leading men of this settlement. He has not been out long from America, but his farm shows what activity will do in a few years. He plants and cultivates corn very extensively. This settlement has land similar to the corn land of Georgia.

Mr. Hart has a very fine farm; he, too, like Rev. White, has not been out from America long enough to have grown rich, but only a few more years are needed to place him among the rich men of the Republic. Mr. Hart cultivates corn and sugar cane very extensively.

Mr. R. J. Richardson, who came from Mississippi in 1895, has one of the most beautiful young farms that I have seen. Mrs. Richardson is a most enterprising lady, and while the husband has been sick and unable to work, yet Mrs. Richardson has succeeded in planting a farm, and in five years they will be on a solid basis.

MARSHALL.

This settlement is generally known as Junk. At this point the Junk River empties into the sea. It is a port of entry and much business is done there. Germans do the most trading.

Rev S T. Prout, of Monrovia, owns some fine property here and does a good business also. Mr. Prout is a young Liberian of thirty-five years. He was educated at the Liberia College and is a local preacher in the M E. Church. He is accumulating a fortune. His family is small and therefore an assistance, not a hindrance.

Rev. J. H. Deputie, who emigrated from Pennsylvania many years ago, was the leading citizen in this settlement. He was presiding elder of St. Paul District and Associate Justice of the Supreme Court of Liberia. He was indeed one of the promoters of the infant Republic, and did much towards building up the cause of education in Liberia, having taught school for many years. He had travelled a great deal, thus adding wide observation to his liberal spirit. He died in March, 1896, full of years and honors.

MONROVIA.

There are many small trading stations and farming settlements not mentioned, which would, if mentioned, brighten this picture; but those who are not better acquainted with Liberia from reading this sketch, or reviewing this picture, are very dull of apprehension.

Monrovia is the national capital; here the President, the ministers and consuls represented at this court, and the cabinet officers, reside. But Monrovia is more than a city of homes; it is a flourishing seaport, and as much business is done here as in the whole Republic besides.

Hon. G. W. GIBSON,
Secretary of State of Liberia.

Hon. ARTHUR BARCLAY,
Secretary of the Treasury of Liberia.

National Government.

Until recently, His Excellency, James Joseph Cheeseman, was President. He was born and educated in Liberia. He came up a poor boy, but had in him the stuff that makes men. His career, till he reached the period of manhood, was not especially noted or brilliant. Being pious from his youth up, he joined the Baptist church before he reached manhood, and early in his twenties he became pastor of the Baptist church at Edina, Bassa County. He was not only a churchman, but was much interested in the government of his country, and soon he was filling the place of clerk in the office of the Collector of Customs. He rose to be the collector and subsequently pushed himself forward to be judge of the quarterly court. This position was filled with much ability.

Having displayed such talent as Judge, he was called to be the chief ruler of the nation. Few Presidents have displayed such executive ability and such power to deal with the native element. When President Cheeseman was elected, war reigned from Cape Mount to Cape Palmas, but in the fifth year of his administration there was peace from one extreme of the Republic to the other. He suggested such legislation as gave the Republic a revenue; money was coined, duties paid and debts cancelled. He bought a gun boat, and by this means kept many steamers from entering ports where there were no collectors of customs. He not only came up step by step in State, but also in Church, until he became the President of the Baptist convention, the highest office in the gift of this church.

But President Cheeseman was also a business man, and one of the leading merchants of Bassa County. He not only accumulated for himself, but felt himself a steward for the Master, and gave much to advance missions among heathens and keep up the educational work of the church. In splendor of dress and carriage there are few courts making greater display than the Court of Liberia. Mrs.

Cheeseman, the wife of the President, is known by all, and gives
great tone to the social side of life.   On fete days she is always on
hand, as pleasant and cheerful as spring time.   She was a Miss Crusoe.
Her father was Liberia's merchant prince in his day.

General Reginald A. Sherman, Ex-Secretary of War and Navy, one
of Liberia's leading statesmen and warriors, whose picture I present,
has had a remarkable career.   He was born in Savannah, Ga., in
1838, and emigrated to Liberia, Africa, with his parents in 1853,
when 15 years old.   He learned the carpenter's trade and worked at
it a number of years, when he was appointed clerk of the court,
which position he satisfactorily filled for two years.   He was appointed collector of customs for the port of Monrovia, to which
office he brought many improvements in the order of business.   This
was during the Presidency of Mr. Benson.   After the expiration of
his term, he was made Treasurer of the Liberian Republic and discharged the duties of the office with credit to himself.

He engaged in mercantile pursuits, and now owns one of the
largest stores in Monrovia, doing a profitable business with England,
France and Germany, and also with the United States through Yates
& Porterfield, from whom one, and often two, vessels with cargoes of
American goods consigned to him, annually arrive.

He became a member of a volunteer company and was soon made
orderly sergeant; was promoted to the office of adjutant, First Regiment, and held this office three years.   In 1862, he was promoted to
the rank of major, in the same regiment, but was soon, by President
Warner, appointed lieutenant-colonel, serving two years.   In 1868,
he was appointed colonel by President Payne.   In 1876 he was
again promoted to the office of brigadier-general, and is now major-
general and Secretary of War and the Navy.

The General has been engaged in many battles and has been
wounded four times.   He has at least once declined the nomination
for the Presidency.

He has a wife, son and daughter.   Mrs. Sherman is a thorough
business woman and most generous in her benefactions to the needy.
She keeps always in store a large quantity of select medicines; is as
much relied upon in sickness as a physician, and is generally successful in treating the ills of the Liberian climate.

The General owns three seacoast sailing crafts and fifteen or more

J. J. CHEESEMAN,
Late President of Liberia

Mrs. J. J. CHEESEMAN,
Widow of President J. J. Cheeseman.

cargo boats, which are used in conveying merchandise to and from steamers in the harbor.   He is financial agent for the Episcopal and Presbyterian missions, and is treasurer of the board of trustees of Liberia College.

He is stern, positive and inflexible, and forward in all measures for the public weal.   His residence, a three-and-a-half story brick mansion, is not excelled by any in the Republic.   He has in course of erection, and nearly completed, another house that promises to rival the one in which he now resides.

He is undoubtedly wealthy, though his modesty restrains him from making any display of his possessions.   He and his family are of a bright or mulatto complexion—a fact showing that persons of color of any shade can live and enjoy good health in Liberia, strict regard being had to the laws of health.

The story of his life, from the slave State of Georgia to the enterprising and wealthy merchant of Liberia, upon whom in the midst of his active business career, have been conferred the highest trusts and honors of his adopted country, would furnish a most valuable lesson and example to the youth of his race.

The present Cabinet are men much above the average.

Secretary of State, Dr. G. W. Gibson, is well advanced in years, and having filled this position several times, is well up in international law and deals readily with knotty diplomatic questions.

Attorney-General F. E. R. Johnson, son of the late President, is a young man, but has travelled much.   He is a student and well fitted for the position.

Secretary of Treasury, Arthur Barclay, is a clever scholar and has been connected with the government many years.   He is therefore the one man that fits in any position.   He is a lawyer by profession.

Dr. J. H. Moore is Secretary of the Interior.   He is a young man; educated in America, and has the ability to fill his position with great credit.   Handsome and entertaining, he makes a social figure that would grace any court.

Hon. A. D. Williams fills the position of Secretary of War and Navy.   There is no man at the Liberian Court more fitted by training for court levees.

Hon. S. J. Dennis fills the important portfolio of Postmaster General.   He is a merchant, the business man of the firm of Dennis

Brothers, wealthy, reserved and intelligent. He is the bachelor of the Cabinet.

This Republic will celebrate its 50th anniversary this year, this being fifty years since the Colonization Society told them to walk alone and they adopted a constitution and elected His Excellency, Joseph J. Roberts, as President. He was an emigrant from Virginia and was President of the infant Republic eight years, being elected four successive times, over all opposition.

GEN. R. A. SHERMAN.
Late General of the Liberian Armies.

At the end of eight years, His Excellency, Stephen A. Benson, became the second President by the choice of the people, he was also elected four times in succession. The President was just the man to follow President Roberts, and for his term of eight years, he accomplished much for Liberia. He took advanced steps and coined money.

In 1864, His Excellency, Daniel B. Warner, was called to the Presidency, but only served two terms. The young men were called to this important office. Presidents Roberts and Benson were only thirty-eight years each, while President Warner was forty-eight years old.

His Excellency, James S. Payne, was elected in 1868, and ably served one term. He was indeed a man of great dignity and ability.

After President Payne had served two years, His Excellency, Edward J. Roye, was elected to be Chief Magistrate, but did not live to serve out one term. He was cruelly deposed by rebels against the government, revolution took the place of law, and the people overthrew the government and set up another with Vice-President James S Smith as chief of the Republic.

After much trouble had occurred, and President Roye had been deposed, His Excellency, Joseph J. Roberts, was elected the second time and re-elected for the second term, and President James S. Payne came to the chair again and served two years, one term only.

But now the older men for counsel were necessary, and His Excellency, Anthony W. Gardner, was chosen to the Presidency in 1878, in the 57th year of his age. He was re-elected in 1880, and again in 1882, but resigned in 1883, and Vice President Alfred F. Russell served out the unexpired term.

When, in 1822, the first little band of Liberian immigrants on Cape Montserrado seemed to be well-nigh overwhelmed with hardship, danger, want, and sickness, in accord with the wishes of the great body of the colonists it was proposed by Dr. Eli Ayres, the United States agent, to abandon the enterprise and return to Sierra Leone, Elijah Johnson, an immigrant from New York, made himself forever famous in Liberian history by his reply: "No; I have been two years searching for a home in Africa, and I have found it; I shall stay here." These heroic words saved the day, and the other colonists remained with him. Dr. Ayres returned to the United States, leaving Elijah Johnson as agent in charge of the colony.

Shortly afterwards, when a number of native petty kings in the neighborhood, who regretted the sale of the cape on account of its interference with the lucrative trade in slaves theretofore carried on from that point, determined to drive these intruders into the sea, and at this critical juncture a British man-of-war in the offing tendered the assistance of a force of marines if Johnson would only cede a little patch of ground on which to erect a British flag, he promptly replied,

"We want no flagstaff put up here that will cost more to get it down than it will to whip the natives."

Hilary Richard Wright Johnson, son of Elijah Johnson, was born in Monrovia, June 1, 1837. The larger part of his training was received in the Alexandria high school, Monrovia, from which institution he was graduated in December, 1857. In January, 1856, and

HILARY RICHARD WRIGHT JOHNSON.
President of Liberia, 1884–1892.

while still attending school, he was appointed private secretary to President Benson, and held the office seven years. In January, 1858, being at the same time private secretary, he was appointed principul of the high school at Day's Hope, Monrovia, and remained in charge until the effects of the civil war in the United States compelled the closing of that institution. In November, 1859, he became editor of the *Liberia Herald*, and conducted that paper for two years and a half. While still private secretary to the President, in 1861, he was elected a member of the House of Representatiyes.

Mr. Johnson attended the International Exhibition in London in 1862, assisted in the discussion of the northwest boundary question,

SUPREME COURT OF LIBERIA,

Chief Justice Hon. R. B. Roberts, Associates Hon. R. B. Richardson and J. J. Dorsen

and, with President Benson, was presented at several European courts. It was during this visit that he made the acquaintance of the old Emperor William, then King of Prussia, Bismarck, Bernstaff, von Buest, and other European statesmen.

In January, 1864, Mr. Johnson was again appointed editor of the *Liberia Herald;* in July of the same year he was elected principal of the preparatory department of Liberia College, and held that post two years and a half. In February, 1865, he was appointed Secretary of State under President Warner, but resigned in July of the same year; he was again appointed Secretary of State under Mr. Warner for 1866 and 1867.

In January, 1867, Mr. Johnson was elected professor of English language, belles-lettres, and mental and moral philosophy in Liberia College, and occupied the chair eleven years. In February of the same year he made, at the instance of Hon. H. M Shieffelin, of New York, a topographical and trigonometrical survey of the "Old Field," with a view of ascertaining the practicability of cutting a canal to connect the Montserrado and Junk rivers. He was appointed Secretary of the Interior under President Roye, in January, 1870. In the same year he visited England and America with the President, and assisted in the discussion of the boundary question in London. On account of a difference of opinion on constitutional questions, he resigned office at the end of the year. He was Secretary of State during the short period of provisional government in 1871. Under the succeeding administration of President Roberts he held the offices simultaneously of Secretary of State and of the Interior (the latter without salary) for the years 1872 and 1873, and then resigned. For the following ten years he declined all offers of positions in the Cabinet.

The degree of Master of Arts was conferred on Mr. Johnson by the board of trustees of Liberia College in 1872, and that of Doctor of Laws in 1882.

In 1877, the representatives of both political parties, as well as the government then in power, offered to support Mr. Johnson for the presidency, but he declined the nomination. When, in 1883, he consented to become a candidate for the presidency, it was the fourth time he had been requested to do so. Having been unanimously elected, he was inaugurated President, January, 1884. He served four terms, or eight years, and declined a fifth nomination, being unwilling to make a departure from what he considered an important precedent.

Besides the classics, Mr. Johnson has made a study of several modern languages. He has also given considerable attention to music, and keeps around him always piano, violin, flute and guitar. As he is able to do his own tuning and repairing, his instruments are always in good order.

Mr. Johnson has had a number of decorations conferred on him by different sovereigns and medals from other sources. He is an honorary member of several foreign societies, of one of which he was elected a member at twenty years of age.

Mr. Johnson has six children. His oldest son, Frederick, when about to proceed on his second visit to Europe, having served the State several years as prosecuting attorney, was last October appointed Attorney General of the Republic. He has had the largest private law practice in the country. Gabriel Moore, the second son, is register of deeds and a captain in the army. His eldest daughter is distinguished for her musical ability and acquirements. She has inherited the talents in this line of both of her parents and is an accomplished performer on the violin, piano and organ.

President Johnson retired from the presidency in 1892, at the age of 55, and since then has devoted himself to farming, especially to coffee raising, and has shown himself to be one of the most intelligent and successful cultivators of the soil in Liberia. The article on "Liberia Coffee" in " Bulletin No. 7," is from his pen.

From all the facts given above, whether we consider him in the light of his scholarly attainments, or his success as a man of affairs; there will be found very few to deny to him the laurels which his statesmanship has placed upon his brow, or to envy him the prosperity which has come to him in this world's goods as the result of foresight and capable administration of his private affairs.

[NOTE.]

It is necessary in order to explain some apparent discrepancies, to state why they appear. The biography and administration of President J. J. Cheeseman and of President Coleman are given on previous pages and are not, therefore, in chronological order, as their administrations form the last two of the Republic, President Coleman being the present executive. As Vice President, under President Cheeseman's administration, he succceded to the presidency on the death of the latter, and has since been elected by popular vote.

It is well to remember also that most of this work was written while I was Minister Resident from the United States to Liberia, while some of the later matter has been prepared since. Thus it will be understood why both sets of facts appear in the present tense, though separated by a period of a year or more.   AUTHOR.

Frederick Grant is a leading merchant and banker in the city of Monrovia.   He rose from a journey worker to a man of great wealth in twenty years.

MR. FREDERICK GRANT
Merchant and Banker of Monrovia, Liberia.

His career is a good example of what push, enterprise and close application to business will do.   In fact, all the instances of prosper-perity mentioned in these pages illustrate, not only the wonderful opportunities and resources of this Republic, but furnish object lessons of the quickness of progressive Liberians to take full advantage of them.

United States Legation.

BY W. B. R.

This Legation is situated in a seven-room building just one square from the President's mansion and not so far from the capitol.

Dr William H. Heatd, our present Minister Resident and Consul General, was born in the United States, in Elbert County State of Georgia, of slave parents, and therefore was a slave until the surrender of Lee to Grant at Appomattox Court House in 1865. He was then in his fifteenth year. But he at once employed private teachers and began for the first time to learn the English alphabet, and in four years he was engaged as one of the public school teachers, which posi tion he filled for twelve years except a part of 1876-77, when he was a member of South Carolina Conference With not more than five years in school, he studied Latin, Greek and Hebrew and the higher mathematics and sciences.

In 1880, he was appointed a railway postal clerk, which position he had the honor of filling with great satisfaction until he resigned to enter fully into the ministry of the A. M. E. Church. He was first appointed to Aiken, S. C. Here he remained two years, during which time a parsonage containing six rooms was built, furnished and every dollar paid thereon. The membership increased two fold.

He was next appointed to Charleston, S. C., where he labored for three years and during his administration more than $16 000 in cash was raised, and three hundred and forty two persons were added to the church. He then took a transfer to Philadelphia, Pa. and was appointed to Allen Chapel, serving only one year. He increased the membership to one hundred and sixty and doubled the congregation, meeting all obligations. He was then promoted to the position of presiding elder of the Lancaster district. He served one year very acceptably, but gave it up to accept the pastorate of the "Mother Church" Bethel, Philada., Pa., serving two years. Twenty-eight

C. MAX MANNING,
Late Secretary of U. S. Legation, Monrovia.

THE SENATE AND OFFICERS OF THE LIBERIAN SENATE.

thousand dollars was collected during this period. Three hundred and sixty members were added to the church. He was then appointed to Wilmington, Del., and so highly were his services appreciated, that at the end of two years, the people protested against his removal. A strong petition was presented from Harrisburg and he was appointed to this charge, but after eight months President Cleveland appointed him Minister Resident and Consul General to Liberia over many competitors, which position he now fills with much ability and pleasure.

Cornelius Maxwell Manning, Secretary of the Legation of the United States at Monrovia, Liberia, is the third and youngest son of Moses and Millie Manning. He was born at Edenton, Chowan County, North Carolina, on Monday, the 8th day of December, 1845. As there was no protection guaranteed to "free Negroes" in those days, the father of our subject moved to Philadelphia when he (Cornelius) was one year old. On account of the impoverished condition of his father, he enjoyed the privilege of the public schools but for a short time. He attended night school, however, and secured such private instructions from time to time as convenience and circumstances would permit. Later in life, he attended the "Institute for Colored Youth," in Philadelphia. He went South with the 3rd New York Artillery during the Civil War, and in 1863 he enlisted as a soldier in Company "K" of what was then known as "The 1st Regiment North Carolina Colored Troops" (Infantry), but was afterward changed to the 35th U. S. C I. In this regiment he served three years, was at the bombardment and final capture of Fort Wagner in 1863, the battle of Olustee, Fla., and Honey Hill, S. C. During the war, our subject applied himself to his books, so that when he was mustered out in 1866, he had mastered Davies' Practical Arithmetic.

He was a member of the constitutional and nominating conventions of North Carolina in 1868, and filled several local positions in his native county.

He attended school at Lincoln University, was licensed to preach in 1873; joined the itinerancy in 1874; was ordained a deacon and an elder in the A. M. E. Zion Church; he was elected to the General Conference of the same church in 1880. He left the Zion and joined the A. M. E. Church in 1881. He served some of the leading churches in the State of Georgia, and spent many years as a school teacher in North Carolina, Alabama and Georgia. He is a shoemaker by trade, though he read law under Judge W. A. Moore, one of the ablest lawyers in Eastern North Carolina.

When appointed to the position which he now holds, he was pastor of Jackson Chapel station, Washington, Georgia, and secretary of the North Georgia Annual Conference of the A. M. E. Church, which position he held four years consecutively.

Hon. Beverly Y. Payne is Vice-Consul. He has acted fully five years since he was appointed and is considered to be very proficient. Mr. Payne is a young man of good business qualities and I do not further describe him because I have done so already.

Mr. Wyatt B Robinson of Atlanta, Georgia, is the messenger; he took his first trip to Liberia in August 1896, and was employed at once in the United States Legation. He is a young man only 22 years of age. He is not an educated young man, having spent the most of his time on a farm.

GERMAN CONSULATE.

The next in importance is the German Consulate. Hon. Herman Jager is the Consul. He has spent twenty years in Liberia as a trader. He lives on Broad street in a large house built of brick. It contains eight or ten rooms. He married within the last year, keeps house and lives in comfort and ease. Mr. Jager is a German, but has the social side of his nature well developed. He is a great friend of Liberia's.

NORWAY AND SWEDEN.

Hon. M. A. Aenmy, who has been in Africa for twenty-five years, is the Consul. He has his office in his house, on the same street with the United States. He married a Mrs. Johns. She died and willed him the house during his life.

NETHERLANDS.

The Netherlands' Consul is Hon. W. W. Barker. Mr. Barker is a merchant and is doing a large business. He lives only a half block from the mansion of the President, to whom he is very much attached.

BELGIUM.

The Belgian Vice-Consul is Hon. Arthur Barclay, who is a Liberian citizen. He is highly fitted for the duties of his position. He lives but one square from the Capitol of the Republic.

HOUSE OF REPRESENTATIVES AND ATTACHES OF LIBERIA.

SPAIN.

Hon. J. R. Cooper is the Spanish Vice-Consul. He is a Liberian, but being a merchant, he is peculiarly fitted for the consulship.

ENGLAND.

Mr. Wring, a merchant who recently came to Liberia trading, is the English Vice-Consul. He is an Englishman.

SUPREME COURT.

This court is now the happy fold in which law and learning reside. Chief Justice Z. B. Roberts, LL.D., is a jurist of no mean standing.

Dr. Robert B. Richardson, who is considered the *literatum* of Liberia, sits on the right hand of the Chief Justice. Justice Richardson is an independent thinker, and many of his dissenting decisions are gems of literature and erudition. He is the leading Baptist divine of Liberia.

Hon. John W. Worrell. This gentleman is the leading lawyer of Bassa County. He came to Liberia from the West Indies more than thirty years ago. He has great learning.

Mr. M. Wims, the marshall, is the peace officer of the court. He is of stature every inch an officer.

Mr. I. J. Sanders is the clerk of the Court. He says very little, but always pays attention to business.

Mr. L. C. Johnson is the assistant clerk. He is unpretentious, but strictly a business man.

The Legislature of the Republic is composed of a Senate and a House of Representatives.

The Senate is composed of Hons. A. B. King and R. H. Jackson, of Montserrado County; Hons. J. D. Summerville and H. B. Williams, of Grand Bassa County; Rev. W. D. Frazier and Hon. J. J. Ross, of Sinoe County; Hons. J. H. Dennis and T. Pratt, of Maryland County. We are giving you the pictures of most of them, in connection with the history of the counties they represent, and a full picture here. The Vice President is President of the Senate—Hon. J. J. Ross, President *ex-officio.*

The House of Representatives is composed of four representatives from Montserrado County and three each from the other three counties.

One of the most intelligent men of the Republic of Liberia, and one who did much towards giving character to the Liberia College, was Henry De Witt Brown, Ph. D.

The county government of Montserrado county is separate and independent, as is that of other counties; yet the National Government oversees it. Now I give you a cut of the Court of Quarter Sessions. Judge Hillary W. Travis presides.

The Court of Probate meets monthly. Judge C. T. O. King is now presiding. We present him and a sketch of his life for our readers.

Judge King was born in Sierra Leone, in 1839. He attended school from early childhood until 1856, when he served as an apprentice at the printer's trade for one year; he then entered the Government printing office, where he was soon promoted to the position of journeyman. Here he remained ten years. In 1867, he was employed as a merchant, and seeing a greater future in a Republic, he removed to Liberia and at once began to fill positions of honor and trust. He was appointed city magistrate, and advanced to Justice of the Peace for Montserrado County. He was afterward Marshal of the Supreme Court of the Republic, Clerk of the Court, Postmaster at Monrovia, Collector of Customs, Secretary of the Interior, a member of the Cabinet and trustee of the Liberia College. After serving these important positions, he was elected Mayor of Monrovia in 1884, and re-elected successively until 1890. During this time, he also served as agent of the Colonization Society of the United States, holding this office until 1892. He was engaged in transplanting Liberian coffee in Brazil, South America, in 1898.

Judge King is Grand Master of the Masons in Liberia, being elected in 1888; he has been retained to the present. He is Judge of the Monthly and Probate Court, and Consul for the Republic of Venezuela, in South America. The judge is one of those spirits which do not see gloom or live in shadows, but he is full of smiles, and at all times lives in the region of sunshine.

The legal profession in Monrovia has some strong men. Secretary Arthur Barclay is a man of vast knowledge and a jurist. Attorney-General Johnson is also a lawyer of keen judicial perception, and has few equals in the Republic. Hon. T. W. Haynes has won his spurs, long since. County Attorney F. W. Ware is a rising young lawyer. Senator J. J. Ross, Representatives Wright and Brooks, Hon. Dawson and Justice Worrell are men whom any court would

COURT OF QUARTERLY SESSIONS, OF MONTSERRADO COUNTY, LIBERIA.

recognize. But we give the sketch of one of the most painstaking, industrious attorneys in Liberia. Clients always feel safe in his hands.

Attorney S. E. F. Cadogan was born in Bridgetown, Barbadoes, West Indies, in 1842, and emigrated to Liberia in 1865. He was Clerk of the Supreme Court for ten years, and Register of Wills and Deeds for nine years. He is a soldier, and rose from the rank of a private to that of captain of the Johnson Volunteers, and then on account of his bravery in war, he was promoted to the rank of brigadier-major, under General Sherman. We present his intelligent face, and when you look upon it, you see a man who fully represents the race, and is a leader at the Liberian capital.

The Merchants of Monrovia.

This class of men is wealthy and independent. To trade is to gain more than one hundred per cent. on the money invested.

The warehouses of H. Cooper & Son extend over acres of terri ory and their profit has been a means of leading to great wealth

J. B. Dennis has just entered the field and is making money

Toles & Co. are merchants who catch much country trade, and turn over their money to great advantage.

W H. King is one of the most conservative of all the merchants on Water street, but he profits at his business.

Dennis Brothers are three young men who are leading others in their trade. They are careful, obliging and competent young men, and are fast growing rich.

Frederick Grant, who came to Liberia from Accra a poor man, less than twenty years ago, is to-day a merchant-prince.

[2] Hill & Moore, who run the largest business in Montserrado county, are also trading at Monrovia, and shipping more ginger and coffee than any Liberian merchant.

R. A. Sherman, after twenty-five years died a merchant-prince.

There are many foreign merchants—German, Dutch, Norwegian and English—besides many Liberian traders on smaller scales. To trade in Liberia is to grow wealthy, the profit is so great.

Montserrado County extends back 240 miles and is 100 front, yet not one-tenth of it is occupied by civilized people. Mt. Coffee is the most interiorward settlement. It is only about 40 miles from the sea.

There is vast wealth in her bowels and forests—iron silver, coal, gold and other metals. There are no woods in the world superior to the rosewood and mahogany. The land, if cultivated, will grow all bread stuffs that do not need frost for development. The fruits of all tropical climes abound here.

PROF. H. D. BROWN.
Late Professor in the Liberia College.

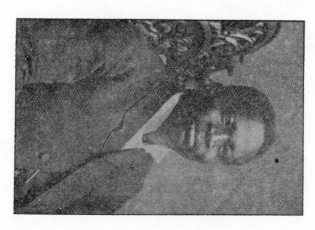

HON. C. T. O. KING.
Grand Master of the Liberian Masonic Order and Judge
of Probate Court, of Montserrado County, Liberia.

But of course there is a need of greater development, and this can only be done as money comes into the Republic by agriculture, mining, trading etc.

The educational facilities are not all they might be. The free schools are about equal to the free schools of Georgia and South Carolina in 1870. But the church schools are doing well. The Episcopalian, Methodist Episcopal, Baptist, Lutheran and African Methodist are all engaged in this work, and the schools follow in the wake of the gospel train. Many native heathen are on board the train.

GRAND BASSA.

This is the second county in importance in the Republic. It was settled in 1842 by emigrants from Montserrado County. These had their conflicts of war and devastation before they could get a foothold. Here the palm-nut, under the discovery of Rev. S. S. Herring, was found to be an article of great value; and trade in this alone soon gave great prominence to this county and many men of ability made their way to this part, for gain. The Cheesemans, Bensons and Herrings were among the leaders – afterward, the Brumskiens, Gardners, Summervilles, Williams, Crusoes, Harrises, Robertses and many others, as Judge J. W. Worrell, of the Supreme Court Bench.

Counties have Governors like the several States of the United States of America, and they are styled Superintendents. The Hon. Joseph D. Summerville is the Superintendent of Grand Bassa County and resides at Lower Buchanan.

Joseph D. Summerville was born in Buchanan, Grand Bassa County, Liberia, May 4, 1860. He did not attend school after he was twelve years of age, but entered a store as a clerk and thus his education was not neglected His employment was among merchants who did much foreign trade. In 1876, when but sixteen years of age, he was superintendent of the business of Messrs. Yates & Porterfield, of New York. In 1882, he was assistant book-keeper in the firm of Messrs. J. Piza & Co., of England. He also made his record as a military man, being captain of the militia when but twenty-three years of age. At the early age of twenty-six years, he was appointed Auditor of Grand Bassa County, by President Johnson, and one year later he was elected a member of the House of Representatives from Grand Bassa. In 1889, he was commissioned Major of the Second Regiment of Liberia, and in the same year he was made superintendent of his county. In the war of 1894, he was Aide to the President at Cape Palmas. He was elected Senator in 1893, served out a full term of four years and was recommissioned by President Coleman, Superintendent of Grand Bassa County He was a brave soldier and for this President Cheeseman knighted him Commander of the Order of African Redemption He is also engaged in business as a merchant and has succeeded. He has a very entensive business at Lower Buchanan, Grand Bassa.

Hon. Henry Byrd Williams is the junior Senator from Grand Bassa County. He was born in the city of Edina, Grand Bassa County, October 13th, 1861. His parents Luther and Elizabeth Williams emigrated from the United States. He was converted and joined the M. E. Church in his seventeenth year. His education was neglected for the want of competent teachers. But he was studious; his mother was his instru tress until 1879, when Prof. A. F Ferguson, A. M., took him in charge. At early manhood his father died and he had to paddle his own canoe. He entered a store as a clerk and then became a factor and agent, but did not remain long at this, for finding he was more adapted to agriculture, he planted a coffee farm and now may be reckoned among the successful farmers of Bassa. In 1886 he entered politics and was appointed Marshal of Grand Bassa. He married Miss Mary A. C Smith in 1886, but was married only one year. He then left Bassa and went to Montserrado and spent two years and six months at Cape Mount. He re-returne 1 to Bassa in 1890 and became clerk to the Collector of Customs; was promoted Collector in 1891. He married the second time in 1893 to Miss N. L Page. He resigned as Collector of Customs in 1895 and assumed the office of Senator which he now fills with much credit. He is the only surviving representative of his family since the death of Secretary Hon. H. A. Williams

Hon. A. J. Woods is one of the representatives of Grand Bassa County He was born in Doyer, Tenn., U. S. A., in 1853 His parents emigrated to Liberia and settled at Grand Cape Mount. His mother did not live long on account of rough treatment at Grand Cape Mount.

Young Woods moved to Monrovia in 1872. He was at the time without means and unemployed; but such men as Hon. H. W. Davis, Mr. I. C. Dickinson and Mr. James Moore gave him their

HON. S. E. F. CADOGAN.
Attorney-at-Law, Monrovia, Liberia.

Hon. J. D. SUMMERVILLE.
Senator from Grand Bassa County.

endorsement, and he was employed by A. Woemann, of Hamburg, trading in Liberia. After one year, they sent him to Grand Bassa as their agent, and he located at Lower Buchanan, there remaining seven years and filling the position with great satisfaction. Being studious, he had read law and was admitted to the bar, leaving A. Woemann.

He began his political life by being elected a member of the Common Council. He was next appointed Judge of the City Court, which position he filled with great satisfaction. He was elected a member of the Lower House of the National Legislature in 1895, and makes an intelligent, progressive representative. Mr. Woods is a young man of wealth.

Before closing the subjects of this important county, I have the pleasure of presenting you the picture of the Major-General of the Republic of Liberia, General I. N Roberts He was born in Georgia, U. S. A., and came to Liberia from Savannah. He is a man of learning and wealth, a lawyer by profession.

The farming districts of Bassa are on the Saint John's River, as they are on the St. Paul River, in Montserrado County. Minerals are picked up on this river as pebbles on a sandy river bed. The resources of this county are unbounded, and it has always been noted for the intelligence of its inhabitants.

The wealthiest merchants that have ever traded in the Republic lived in Bassa, the Crusoes and Attiers. These men were worth more than a quarter of a million, and accumulated all in less than a quarter of a century from the raw materials of this undeveloped country. The opportunity is not less to-day.

Sinoe County is farther south, and has not been developed as Bassa has. Emigrants have not entered this county to any great extent, therefore the natives make up the population. The Representatives are equal to any in the Republic.

Senator J. J. Ross, whose cut we give, was born in Augusta, Georgia, U. S. A., December, 1841. His mother died when he was an infant ; he emigrated to Liberia and settled in Sinoe when but eight years of age. He attended school until he was fifteen years old, when the Sinoe War closed the schools. He entered the war, and when it ended, his grandmother gave him to Mr. William H. Harvey, of Grand Bassa County. This man was a hard master, and taught young Ross only to labor ; he did not see a school nor church except in passing.   But his stay in Bassa was short, only seven months.   His grandmother was dead and buried when he returned to Sinoe ; he was bound out as an apprentice to C. L. Parsons, Esq., who has since been elevated to Chief Justice of the Republic of Liberia.   He sent young Ross to school, where he made rapid strides until he was eighteen years of age, when he was again put at menial labor.   Judge Parsons returned to the United States.

Senator Ross was retained a year in the Bush country and learned to speak Kroo as fluently as a Krooman.   His apprenticeship expired in 1861.   He entered the army and went to Cape Palmas, the seat of war.   On his return to Sinoe he entered the law office of Chief Justice Z. B. Roberts and was admitted to practice in 1864.   He was defeated for the House of Representatives in 1869.   Later he was appointed Judge of the Common Pleas.   In 1875 he was appointed Governor of Sinoe County.   In 1878 he was elected Senator of Sinoe. He visited England and the United States in 1880.   In 1882 he was a member of President Gardner's Cabinet, holding the folio of Attorney General.   He was re-elected Senator of Sinoe County in 1884. He was again a member of the Cabinet under President Johnson in 1888 as Attorney General, and re-elected to the Senate again in 1893. He is now President *pro tem.* of the Senate.   President Cheeseman, in 1895, conferred upon Senator Ross the title of "Knight Commander of the Liberian Humane Order of African Redemption." Senator Ross is a man of family, he has one grown son, a lawyer. He is one of the wealthiest men in Sinoe.

The junior Senator of Sinoe County is Hon. D. W. Frazier.   He has not been many years from South Carolina, U.S.A.   He finished his studies at Lincoln University, then came out here as a Presbyterian missionary.   He entered at once into politics and the people took hold of him and elevated him.   He is a man of intelligence and push, and by that means, he has a national reputation.   He resides at Greenville, Sinoe County, and has accumulated some wealth.   The future in Liberia reserves much for Hon. D. W. Frazier.

His Honor, Z. B. Roberts, Chief Justice of Liberia, is an inhabitant of Sinoe County.   He was born in Savannah, Georgia, U.S.A., 1834.   He emigrated to Liberia with his parents and eight other children in 1840; they settled in Sinoe Country.   He had learned the

Hon. A. J. WOODS.
Representative of Grand Bassa County, Liberia.

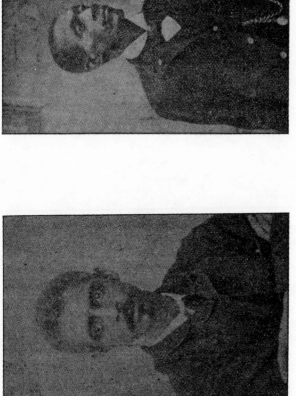

Senator H. B. WILLIAMS.
Of Grand Bassa County, Liberia.

cooper's trade and at once began the operation of his trade. In 1853, his father, Rev. Isaac Roberts, put him in school in Grand Bassa County. In 1855, he was called home to help quell the native uprising. He was appointed Adjutant of the Second Regiment, by Colonel I. D. Washington.

After peace was declared, or the enemy was vanquished, he returned to Grand Bassa County to school, and prosecuted the study of Theology. In 1858 he was ordained and installed pastor of the Greenville Baptist Church, Sinoe County. After several years, of a successful pastorate, he began the study of law, and was admitted to the bar. In 1863 his popularity in standing by the poor at the bar, elected him a member of the Lower House of the General Assembly, and he was re-elected in 1865. He was promoted to the Senate in 1868; he was again returned to the Senate in 1874. He is a lover of his race and country, and did much in this direction while a member of the Legislature. President Gardner knighted him for meritorious services to his country. He was also County Attorney and Commissioner of Native Africans, was Judge of the Court of Common Pleas, was appointed Associate Justice of the Supreme Court by President Russell in 1884. President Cheeseman appointed him Chief Justice in 1895 upon the retirement of Chief Justice Parsons, who lost his sight.

Chief Justice Roberts preaches and acts as pastor of Greenille M. E. Church; he has a mission up the Sinoe He is a mineralogist, and this country abounds in precious metals ; the Chief Justice has a fine collection. He is engaged in the timber business.

Sinoe has some of the finest woods in Africa—cedar and mahogany. Her exports of mahogany are extensive. Up the Sinoe River coffee farms abound. As up the Saint Paul in Monserrado, and Saint John's in Grand Bassa, so it is up the Sinoe.

The Chief Justice wears with dignity and grace the titles of LL.D., and D.C.L.

These public men, with the Haineses, make this county what it is. Its possibilities are not easily depicted, so much lies in the soil and forest untouched. This country greatly needs immigrants, for the Bisshe people are very annoying, and they are warlike and hard to be kept in subjection; often they rise up and are only conquered by severe treatment.

Maryland is the county settled by the Maryland Colonization Society. It is thinly populated with the Liberian Americans, yet the natives have been assimilated and many of them are intelligent citizens, and fill offices of trust and honor. The tribes that inhabit this county are more courageous than any of the tribes, leaving out the Mandingoes. They have been educated by the missionary effort of Bishop L. D. Ferguson of the Protestant Episcopal Church, and are more than a match for the Liberians ; for they are much more numerous. They may be naked, but many of them have good educations. Bishop Ferguson has been and is a benefactor to Liberia. Through him, Maryland holds the leading place in an educational sense. The Methodist Church and the government have expended their efforts on Montserrado County. But they have worked spasmodically, while the Episcopals have worked methodically. This County, like all of Africa where emigrants are few, has failed to develop the resources or till the land, yet there are many farmers of note in Maryland, and coffee is being exported extensively.

This county is represented in the Legislature by Senator Pratt, as the senior Senator. He is from Sierra Leone, well educated and about fifty years of age. He is one of the most faithful officials in the Republic. Like Judge C. T. O. King, he is indeed conscientious and trustworthy. He fills this important office with dignity and ability.

Senator James H. Dennis is the junior Senator. He was born in the City of Harpers, Maryland County, May, 1862. His father, James B. Dennis, emigrated from the State of Maryland, U. S. A., in 1833, and settled in Montserrado County. The next year he and twenty-nine others volunteered to open up a new county at Cape Palmas. His mother, Ann E. Dennis, was also from the State of Maryland. The Hon. James H. Dennis is the youngest of eight children. He has been brought up under the religious influence of the Protestant Episcopal Church, and educated by their missionaries, Bishop S. D. Ferguson himself being his instructor. The war of 1874 caused his parents to emigrate to Montserrado County, and young James was taken away from the schools of Cape Palmas ; yet he was not left entirely without educational opportunities, for he attended a primary school during this time, and after the close of the war in 1877, he returned to Cape Palmas. After two years he entered the mercantile business.

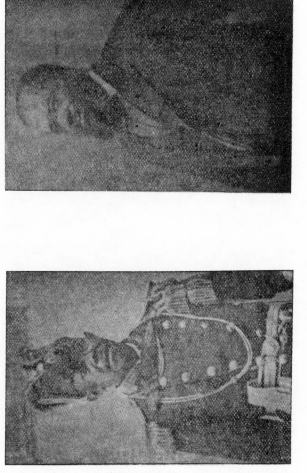

Late Lieut. Gen'l I. N. ROBERTS.
Of Grand Bassa County, Liberia.

Vice-President J. J. ROSS.
Of Sinoe County, Liberia.

In 1887, under Bishop Ferguson, he began teaching in the Caballa River settlement as a catechist in the Protestant Episcopal Church. He entered the militia of his county and was commissioned captain in 1892; he also served ·the government, having been appointed County Auditor in the same year. The next year, he was nominated and elected a member of the Lower House of Representatives of the Liberia Legislature. He began politics in the Whig party and continues a member of that party.

His ability and love of country continued his elevation, so that in 1895 he was nominated for senator, but Hon J. J. Brewer beat him four votes on the face of the returns. The Whigs, however, being in the majority, Senator Brewer was unseated and the seat given Senator Dennis, who fills the position with much ability. He is honest, intelligent and patriotic.

The House of Representatives is composed of men who rank in intelligence and patriotism with any in the Republic.

Hon. James L. Cox was born in Maryland County, Republic of Liberia, June, 1854. His father was an emigrant from America; he was the father of six children, James being the oldest son. He entered school at an early age, but his father did not live to see him educated, so he left school before completing his education to look after the support of his father's family when only sixteen years of age. He learned the trade of a sawyer, and thus obtained means working at his trade to support his mother. He enlisted in the war of 1875 between the Greboes and Liberian government. He was wounded, but as soon as his wound was healed, he was found in line against the enemy.

In 1884, he was commissioned a Justice of the Peace. He was promoted in two years and made Sheriff of Maryland County. He was again called into line against the old enemy in 1893. His patriotism gave him prominence among the people, and in 1894, he was elected a member of the National Legislature.

Hon. Frederick Wiley (Tobo) Proud, whose sketch and cut we give, was born of aborigines. His father, John Greene (Tobo) Proud, was converted to Christianity and joined the Protestant Episcopal Church at the age of twenty-five, under the preaching of Rev. C. C. Hoffman, at Cape Palmas. His mother was given to Bishop Payne when only six years of age, but it was understood that she should return to her father, who was " Grand Devil" of the " Devil

Bush," after she was educated. Her father lived on the Cavalla River, but after she was educated, she refused to return to heathenism and was married to John G. Proud ; their union brought three children, two girls and one boy.

Young Proud lost his father when he was but four years of age. He was taken into the Protestant Episcopal Church at Cape Palmas, and completed his studies at Hoffman Institute under the tutorship of the late Rev. M. P. K. Valentine.   He was licensed a lay reader in 1884, and employed as a catechist on the Cavalla River.   He is organist of St. James P. E., Church, Cape Palmas, and Secretary of the vestry, besides being superintendent of the Sabbath school.   He entered politics and was elected a Representative in 1895   He is a farmer and a man of means.

There is no county in the Republic where the possibilities are greater.   The minerals hidden in the earth here in this wild country are rich and rare; diamonds and gold abound.

More has been done to educate the aborigines and assimilate them with the body politic in this country than elsewhere.

The debt of gratitude due Bishop S. D. Ferguson, D.D., D.C. L., by Liberia, will not soon be canceled, for he has done more to educate and christianize the native than any one man in the Republic. For more than thirty years this man of God has labored constantly. Many have labored as assiduously, but they had facilities and the means to do the work.

The enterprising American is invited to turn his eye toward this field.   The farmers of Maryland County are not numerous, but they are successful and much coffee is being shipped from this part.

Hon. J. H. DENNIS.
Senator from Cape Palmas.

Hon. JAMES L. COX.
Representative of Maryland County.

Missionary Efforts In Liberia.

The Protestant Episcopal Church, under the management of Rt. Rev. S. D. Ferguson, D.D., D.C.L., has done more than any denomination in lifting the heathen into civilization and Christianity.

Rt. Rev. Samuel David Ferguson, D.D., D.C.L., was born in the city of Charleston, South Carolina, U. S. A., January 1st, 1842. His parents (Edward and Elizabeth Ferguson) brought him to Liberia at the age of six years, with two other younger children, taking up their residence in Greenville, Sinoe County. Within six months after their arrival, his father and both sisters departed this life. To be left with a widowed mother, without pecuniary means, is a calamity to be dreaded anywhere; how much more in a country like this nearly a half century ago. Fortunately, the father set to work providing a home for his family immediately after his arrival, and had succeeded in erecting a dwelling house. But that was all; and so the widow and her son passed through many hardships Although so young,, Samuel did all in his power to lighten his mother's burden. He was her factotum. Hewing wood, drawing water. scrubbing, cooking and the like, fell to his lot, and he has always been proud to say that he lost nothing by it. This continued until he was entering his sixteenth year, when his mother, taking into consideration the necessity of having her son prepared for future life resolved to deny herself of his service and so placed him with the Rev. Hezekiah Greene, a colored missionary from the United States of America,who had recently been placed in charge of the Episcopal Church of Greenville, and who taught a first-class school. Up to this time Samuel had attended the public schools. This was an important epoch in his life.

A few months later he made an outward profession of religion, having been piously inclined all his life, and was subsequently confirmed in the Episcopal Church by the late Bishop John Payne. His teacher noticed him closely, and, at that early age, in conversation with his friends, predicted that he would become a bishop. Considering that no Negro had ever been elevated to such a position in the Protestant Episcopal Church, and that there seemed at that time no probability of such an occurrence, this was quite a venture of faith on his part. To Samuel, of course, no event would have seemed more unlikely; but he was evidently in the path to promotion of some kind. From the day that he ratified and confirmed the promises that had been made in his name at his baptism in infancy, he felt a strong inclination to work for God, which has never left him. Of his own accord he organized a weekly prayer-meeting among the boys with whom he associated ; which was regularly held until he left Sinoe. He obtained permission to spend one of his vacations with a friend of his mother at Nanna Kroo, a native village on the coast, fifteen miles from Greenville. There were only two civilized families there. and he was thus brought in direct contact with heathen life. Walking in the village on one occasion, his attention was directed to an aged man lying sick in his hut. He went in, spoke to him about the Great Physician and knelt in prayer by his side. Regular visits were afterwards made to the village for gospel work. Thus at the age of sixteen was the missionary spirit kindled in his soul, and the fire has never gone out.

Such was his progress in school, his teacher, Mr. Greene, decided to send him to the Mt Vaughan High School at Cape Palmas, which has been recently opened by the Episcopal mission and placed in charge, of the Rev. Dr. Alexander Crummell. It was a regular boarding school. On his arrival there, he had just entered his seventeenth year. Everything was now quite new and strange to him—no mother near, no familiar faces; but God was there and he had learned to confide in Him. Four hours a day with the hoe, beginning at 5 a. m., seemed awfully hard, especially as painful blisters were at first raised in his hands; but he soon got all right, and could cut as much grass and throw up as many potato ridges with the hoe as the next boy. He was soon made a monitor, and then had not only to do his own work, but to see that the other boys did theirs.

Dr. Crummell was a good teacher, and Samuel gained much from him. One of the white missionaries, who had lived at Cape Palmas and returned to the United States, (the Rev. H. H. Messenger) on hearing of his advancement to the episcopal office, wrote a letter

BISHOP H. M. TURNER,
Bishop to Africa of the A. M. E. Church.

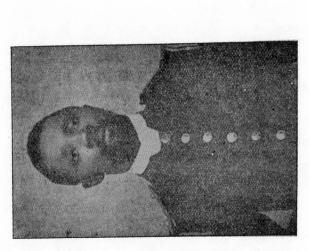

Hon. G. W. PROUD.
Representative of Maryland County, Liberia.

which was published in a periodical of the Board, stating, among other things, that he was not surprised at his success from what he had witnessed at the examinations of the school.

After two years, he was permitted to visit his home and mother. While there, volunteers were called for to join a military expedition that was being raised to wage war againt a disloyal heathen tribe near Cape Palmas. He enlisted, was made seargeant major, and went through the campaign. It is known as the Padee war.

He returned to school after having been discharged from military duties, and a few months later (1862), received a call from the late Bishop John Payne to teach the boys' boarding school at Cavalla, the then headquarters of the Mission, twelve miles below Cape Palmas. His connection with the Mission as a worker dates from this, at the age of twenty. He was thus employed a little less than a year, when, on the resignation of Mr. J. B. Yates, the gentleman who succeeded Dr. Crummell at Mt. Vaughan High School, the Bishop placed him in charge of that institution, his *alma mater*. Such a position tested his metal. There he had control of young men who had been, his schoolmates, and he was still under age. He succeeded in commanding respect, and his executive ability was soon developed. Having the care of the household, he sent for his mother and was privileged to have her spend her remaining days with him, which were not many; for she died soon after he attained his majority and on the eve of his marriage.

He continued in charge of that institution about ten years—until its removal to another locality. His time was then devoted solely to his clerical work; he having been ordained to the diaconate by Bishop Payne on the 31st of December, 1865, and to the priesthood by the same prelate, three years later, and placed in charge of St. Mark's church, Cape Palmas. For thirty-two years he ministered to this flock, which grew and prospered under him. Several parochial organizations engaged in the work of spreading the gospel manifest the life of the church. He regrets having now to resign the care of this parish owing to the necessity of devoting his whole time to the duties of the Episcpal office.

He made his first visit to the United States in 1874, and had the honor of being the first colored clergyman of the Episcopal Church seen in his birthplace—Charleston, S. C. He officiated in St. Mark's church (colored), which was under a white pastor. They gave him a public reception and made him a present of a black silk gown. His relatives and the old friends of his parents spared no pains to make his visit an agreeable one.

Some time after his return to the field, he was made Treasurer of the Mission under the administration of the Rt. Rev. Dr. Penick, the third missionary bishop; which position he filled up to the time of his departure for the United States at the call of the church for consecration. His accounts, regularly forwarded to the Board in New York, were always spoken of with commendation. Said Bishop Penick in one of his published letters to the Board, "I find Mr. Ferguson a correct business man.''

In 1884, when the House of Bishops assembled in the city of New York to elect a Bishop for the missionary jurisdiction of Cape Palmas and parts adjacent, the successful career of the subject of this sketch led to his receiving the call, although it involved a new departure in having a Negro member of that august body. On the the 24th of June, 1885, he was duly consecrated in Grace Church in the city of New York, U. S. A.

I have given the above sketch of the life of Bishop Ferguson, that the public might know the man who has done and is doing so much to civilize, christianize and citizenize the Greboe tribes—a people mighty in war and successful in peace. It will be seen from the life of Frederick W. (Tobo) Proud that they are readily engrafted into the body politic. The government of this county is in the hands of the Christian churchmen, and they are trying to so mete out justice that the heathen might receive his portion.

This denomination dots this county with schools and churches. It has one church in Sinoe County, two in Bassa County, and several in Montserrado; and wherever they have the church, they have the school house also. We present St. Mark's Church, of which Bishop Ferguson is rector. Here he spent his best days.

BISHOP SAMUEL D. FERGUSON, D.D.
of the P. E. Church, Cape Palmas, Liberia,

Denominations in Liberia.

THE METHODIST EPISCOPAL CHURCH.

The Methodist Episcopal Church, under the Rt. Rev. J. C. Hartzell, D.D., is doing much in civilizing and feeding the civilized with spiritual food.   Bishop Hartzell, having spent many years in the Southern States among the Negroes, is therefore fitted for the African work, but a Negro is preferred by a majority of the people to any white man.   His missionary draft does much in making him acceptable.   But the Bishop's heart is in the work, and he has entered it with zeal.   His church is doing something in an educational sense worthy of commendation.

Bishop Hartzell is below medium height and rotund in personage. Physically, he is stout and compact; keen-eyed, expressive of a perceptive mind; fatherly and firm in disposition.

Under this consecrated man, Methodism as represented by the M. E Church, is taking on new life.   She extends from Cape Palmas to Cape Mount, but few of her men are equal to the task of presenting the gospel intelligently.   The older men, who came from America prepared for this Christian duty, have all gone, some here and others there.   In many cases, those left have more than they can attend, being national or state officials.   This church has done much in Montserrado County in educating and christianizing.   But while the missionaries have held important stations, the work under white missionaries does not spread rapidly.   There is one missionary in Monrovia who has given more than fifteen years' services among the Kroo people, but her converts may be counted on the fingers, for trading and money getting has interested some of these white missionaries more than soul saving. The goods furnished the missionaries from abroad are sold, and the money banked in America as the individual savings of the missionary.   If the M. E. Church has failed, it is along this line, for Bishop Taylor allowed some of this class to impose on his godly judgment.

THE PRESBYTERIAN CHURCH.

This denomination has accomplished much in the interior and on the St. Paul River.

Rev. J. R. M. Deputie has been the leading spirit in this work. At Careysburg he has managed a first-class school and he has also administered the word of life.

Hon. A. B. King and wife have conducted a school at Clay Ashland for several years.

Rev. D. W. Frazier has managed most successfully a mission at Greenville, Sinoe county,

Other clergymen have labored among the heathen, at the capital of the Republic. The Presbyterians have a comfortable house of worship.

THE BAPTIST DENOMINATION.

This denomination is among the most prosperous, self-supporting in the Republic of Liberia.

The late President J. J. Cheeseman was president of the Baptist Convention for many years. His life was given in building up his church. He said "I have no children, I have adopted Liberia, and my time and money shall be spent in building up this Republic."

He further said that the schools for the Baptist denomination should never suffer while he had means, as he could not help Liberia in a way better than educating the youth and christianizing the heathen. The church had great confidence in him. He was the leader of that denomination. Ricks Institute, with her score of students and half dozen teachers, attests his ability; this school is run without foreign aid. We have given his picture and life elsewhere.

Rev. Robert B. Richardson, D.D., the Secretary of the Baptist Convention and President of Ricks Institute, one of the most learned and eloquent ministers in Liberia, and has been and is to-day a mighty force in building up this church and her educational interests. Dr. Richardson is Associate Justice of the Supreme Court of Liberia, has shown much depth of learning and self-reliance. His dissenting opinions show independence of thought and legal ability and prove him to be second to no man on the bench.

Rev. June Moore, who is Vice-President of the Baptist Convention is not a man of great education, but he is a man of great natural ability. He came from South Carolina about twenty years since and

PROTESTANT EPISCOPAL CHURCH OF HARPER'S, CAPE PALMAS.
Bishop S. D. Ferguson, D.D., Rector.

has accumulated a fortune in twenty years. This fortune has been
the means of assisting the Baptists in this Republic in doing more to
educate and christianize the heathen than many other denominations.
There are many wealthy men in the Baptist church who have given
liberally.

Revs. J. O. Hayes has done much toward -educating and christianizing the heathen. He is from North Carolina. Rev. M. Worrell
was also a power in his day. Rev. J. A. Johnson is now doing much
in Monrovia as pastor of Providence Baptist church. This denomination is self-supporting, and yet it is as successful as any other financially.

THE AFRICAN METHODIST EPISCOPAL CHURCH.

This denomination was planted in Liberia about seventeen years
ago, by Revs. S. F. Flegler, Clement Irons and S. J. Campbell.
These labored and gave the A. M. E. Church a foothold. After a
After a few years, Rev. S. F. Flegler returned to South Carolina and
there has since prosecuted his work. Rev. Irons remained in Africa
and continued to build up the A. M. E. Church, until to-day her
buildings dot the Republic and her members are numerous.

Rev. J. S. Campbell, after many years, left the African Methodist
Church and joined the Presbyterian. Many younger men from America have joined the ranks in Liberia. Rev. T. R. Geda came out, but
did not live to accomplish much. Rev. Vreeland followed; his life
was cut short. Rev. A. L. Ridgel followed, and being strong and
accomplished, he lived more than two years, and they were years that
told in advancing African Methodism; no one has done more.

Dr. William H. Heard, United States Minister Resident, being a
minister in this church, lent his services to build up the church. Rev.
C. Max Manning, A.M., being Secretary of the Legation of the
United States and an elder in the A. M. E. Church, put in many
solid blows in helping to advance the Redeemer's kingdom under this
banner. Rev. L. C. Curtis, a student from Howard University, was
the next to follow; he at once entered upon his duties as Presiding
Elder, and showed his great love for souls and his unbounded zeal
for the elevation of the race. Revs. Lindsay, White, Lewis, Bailey,
Brisbane, the Grosses and others are engaged in building up a race
church. It is the composition of the church that makes it take in
Africa. At its head are Negroes.

The Rt. Rev. Henry McNeil Turner, D.D., LL.D., D.C.L., who is the Senior Bishop of this church, made his first visit to Liberia in 1891, and has repeated this visit twice.

Bishop Turner has few equals in the literary world. He is a scientist of deep research, and a philosopher of keen perception. He does not take a back seat as a linguist, and as a philosopher his equal must be hunted among the ripest scholars. Our subject was born in Columbia, South Carolina, sixty years ago. His parents were free people, consequently he never was a slave; but he remained in this slave State until he reached manhood, and therefore was deprived of educational facilities. After he reached his majority, he left South Carolina and went to Baltimore to take charge of a church. Here he labored and studied until he had mastered the rudiments of an English education, and could read Latin, Greek and Hebrew. He also pastored a church in Washington, D. C., and here he acquired more education. When the War of the Rebellion broke out between the States, he was the first Negro commissioned as a chaplain in the army. He remained in the army until the war ended. Afterwards he was commissioned to go South as a Moses and lead his people, politically and religiously. He was a member of the Constitutional Convention during the Reconstruction period, and also a member of the Legislature. He preached on Sundays, and received into the church over thirty thousand persons, and licensed nearly a thousand ministers to preach the gospel.

From class leader, he has held every position in the church, with a membership of over 600,000, until he became its Senior Bishop.

THE A. M E. ZION CHURCH.

The A. M. E. Zion Church has had a footing in Liberia for more than fifteen years. Rev. A. Cartwright has been the pioneer. The church has not grown rapidly. There is a good school at Brewersville and one church; but this one church, with its pastor and his intelligent wife, has added its quota to advance the heathen and spread the Redeemer's kingdom.

MISSIONARIES.

The missionaries are so many traders, in most of Africa, except those who are regularly appointed. Many of these irresponsible missionaries are engaged in the "down lifting" of the natives. They receive money, provisions, clothing, etc., from philanthropic friends

ELIZA TURNER MEMORIAL A.M.E. CHAPEL, MONROVIA.
REV. W. H. HEARD. D. D.
Pastor.

THE FIRST A. M. E. CHURCH IN MONROVIA, LIBERIA.

in England and America; all of these are sent for the benefit of the mission, but they are sold by many of the white missionaries for the benefit of their personal fund. Many are in Africa as suffering missionaries, who are growing rich as merchants. Mission goods are all admitted free of duty, so the missionary, not paying duty, undersells the merchant and yet makes a greater profit, as the goods do not cost the missionaries anything. Many of the white missionaries are a libel upon Christianity. I speak from knowledge.

Liberia's Future and the Negro's Opportunity.

Much for her future depends on the men who stand at the head of affairs Her past is a demonstration of the Negro's ability to give her a future. She needs strong, patriotic men at the helm of State. It is a wonder she has existed so long as a nation under existing circumstances, but strong men have held her in the place of national recognition. These men are more needed for the future than they were in the past.

The emigrant is the important factor in Liberia's future. The diplomate has the grandest opportunity to display his knowledge of international law and government. The lawyer may here prove his ability as a jurist and earn golden laurels. The physician may display skill in healing a malady that carries thousands to untimely graves, and thus give a home to many white men, who would gladly go to Africa and make it their home, but life is too uncertain there at present. The merchant may reap a reward for his genius here, undreamed of elsewhere. The minister may gather a harvest such as will meet the approval of a just God. The farmer may grow wealthy in fifteen years growing coffee, while he ekes out a miserable existence in the United States. The harvest is white ; opportunities are unparalleled in any other country in the civilized world, especially for the Negro.

The domestic system of slavery, practiced by many people, is a blot upon Liberia's fair name ; many believe slavery, as practiced, a blessing to the natives and a means of civilization.

THE QUARTERLY DRILL OF THE FIRST AND SECOND REGIMENT
Of Liberia. Gen. J. D. Jones, Col. J. B. Dennis, Col. B. Y. Payne.

The Aborigines.

The Kroo dwarf men are the navigators and live in towns along the coast. They are most shrewd and least intelligent. They do not take to American habits nor language. Here we present a Kroo woman.

The next tribe of note is the Greboes. They are intelligent, warlike and full of business principles They do not easily submit to a foreign yoke. They have given Liberia much trouble and fought two wars of note.

The Veys are also a people of high qualities, and do not give up ancient customs and habits without a struggle. In and around Cape Mount they carried on a war for ten years. Their language is akin to the Arabic.

The Mandingoes are the most active, intelligent and business-like of all the tribes. They are clothed and religious ; most of them are Mohammedans. I fail to show the Bassa tribe, Hurrah, Dey, Gallah and Pessah tribes; they are the domestics and slaves, including the Congoes. There are many interior tribes of rare characteristics, not mentioned, as the Baolines, etc.

To Musardu and Return to Boporu.

This journey is a romance in real life, by Benjamin J. K. Anderson, Sr.

Mr. Anderson was born in the city of Baltimore, U. S. A., sixty-three years ago. He is a man of strong physique, and wears well. He does not look to be over forty-five years of age. His equal as a mathematician is not roaming the streets in every cross-road town in any country.

Mr. Anderson has taught mathematics in the Liberia College, is the surveyor of Montserrado County, and has filled the position of Secretary of the Treasury. His journey was the result of funds furnished by Mr. Henry M. Schieffelin, of New York, U S. A., through President D B. Warner, of Liberia. Such enterprises would open up the interior, and do more to advance trade than anything else, besides civilizing the heathen.

Musardu is the capital of the Western Mandingoes, and in French territory. This tribe of people has always excited the liveliest interest, on account of their intelligence, activity and religious proclivities. They are superior to their fellows. Mr. Anderson was supplied with the following instruments: one sextant, by E. and G. W Blunt, of New York; one aneroid barometer; two thermometers, by Pike and Hunter, of New York; one watch, and one artificial horison. Mr. Anderson took a canoe and had carriers. He left Monrovia, February 14, 1868, and went six miles up the St. Paul River, from whence he was carried overland to Musardu. His chief interpreter, Kaifal Kanda, a Mandingo, led the way, for he knew all the country. The journey is described as follows:

This account of a journey to Musardu, the capital of the Western Mandingoes, is the result of a proposal made by Henry M. Schieffelin, of New York, through President D. B. Warner, of Liberia, who for six or eight years had been endeavoring, till now without success, to induce the inauguration of an expedition from Liberia, to explore

A VEY WOMAN.

A KROO WOMAN.

the interior as far as possible. Mr. Schieffelin and Caleb Swan, Esq., of New York, furnished the means necessary to carry on the exploration.

No especial point was indicated by the promoters of this exploration; only the general direction was given, east and northeast. The especial point, however, agreed upon by my friends in Monrovia, was Musardu, the capital of the Western Mandingoes. This is the portion of the country of Manding which our citizens Seymour and Ash attempted to visit; but their travels were unfortunately interrupted in a manner that nearly cost them their lives.

The Mandingoes have always excited the liveliest interest on account of their superior physical appearance, their natural intelligence, their activity, and their enterprise. No one has passed unnoticed these tall black men from the eastern interior, in whose countenances spirit and intellect are strongly featured.

Their diligent journeys from Tallakondah have allowed no seacoast town north-west of the St. Paul's to remain unvisited. Their avidity for trade has drawn them from their treeless plains to the Atlantic ocean. Their zeal for Islam has caused the name of Mohammed to be pronounced in this part of Africa, where it otherwise would never have been mentioned.

Musardu can, by easy journeys, be reached from Monrovia in twenty-five or thirty days. I was obliged, however, from the delays and inconveniences incident to interior traveling in Africa, to occupy thirteen months.

Sometimes I was compelled to spend considerable lengths of time in one place. I have not on that account burdened this report with insipid recitals of what, every day, nearly repeated itself. Whatever struck me as descriptive of the country, or illustrative of the manners of the people, that I have recorded.

I am sensible that the regions through which I have traveled are capable of yielding vaster stores of information, in a scientific point of view, than what I have afforded; but I shall be satisfied if this humble beginning succeeds in encouraging others in the same direction, and on a more extensive scale. I shall now proceed to narrate the journey from Monrovia to Musardu; but especially from Boporu to Musardu.

I shall rapidly march through the two grand divisions of the Boozie country. I shall first make the reader acquainted with the Domar

Boozie, introduce him at once to the populous and thriving towns of Zolu, Zow-Zow, Salaghee, Fissahbue, and Bokkasaw. Leaving the Domar country, we shall enter the Wymar country give time to rest at Ziggah Porrah Zue, in latitude 8° 14′ 45″, its capital, the vast and noisy market of which takes place every Sunday, upon the banks of the same river on which Clay Ashland, Louisiana, Virginia, and Caldwell are seated—the St. Paul's. We shall then cross that river upon a suspension bridge of wicker-work elevated twenty-five feet from its surface, and come into the territory of one of the most war-

GREBOE WOMAN.

like kings in the Wymar country, the bloody Donilnyah. We shall not tarry long in his presence, but, hastening away, nothing shall stop our progress—not even the Vukkah mountains, a boundary acknowledged to divide the fertile hills of Womar from the almost treeless plains of Manding. Crossing these with the tramp and speed of a soldier, we shall quickly descend into the country of the Western Mandingoes; visit their principal cities; and, finally, take up our abode in their very capital—Musardu.

The instruments with which observations were made were: One

MANDINGOE PEOPLE.

sextant, by E. & G. W. Blunt, New York; one aneroid barometer; two thermometers—1st, 133°; 2d, 140°, by B. Pike, New York; two small night and day compasses, by H. W. Hunter, New York; one tolerably good watch; one artificial horizon.

As for the accuracy of these calculations of latitude and longitude, whatever painstaking and the instruments enumerated above could do, has not been neglected.

I have not been able to calculate the profile of the route according to the usual methods, because it was impossible to procure the proper instruments, with which a contemporaneous register ought to have been kept at Monrovia, during my absence.

Even the barometer with which I was furnished was an aneroid, an instrument that has to be referred from time to time to the mercurial barometer for adjustment.

I can not say that the indications of the instrument were material departures from the truth. It certainly indicated the rise and fall of land in a satisfactory and unmistakable manner, both in going to and returning from Musardu.

At Totoquella, in latitude 7° 45′ 24″, and Boporu, June 9th and 13th, it ranged 29.36, 29.34. Upon my return in March it ranged from 29.14 to 29.24. This difference may be ascribed, partly to difference of seasons of rains and dries, and partly to want of accuracy in the instrument itself.

I was not even able to ascertain directly the several heights of land by means of the boiling point of water, because my thermometers ranged only from 133° to 140° Fahrenheit. The highest rise of land was indicated by the aneroid at 27.61 inches; the boiling point of which would have been 208° Fahrenheit. See Davies & Peck's Mathematical Dictionary, page 338, "Table of barometric heights corresponding to difference of temperature of boiling water." It is from these tables that I have made approximate estimates of the elevations of land.

Taking the indications of the aneroid at the several places, and ascertaining from the tables the boiling points at each place, (which always rated higher than my two thermometers of 133° and 140° Fahrenheit,) I then made the calculation as if I had ascertained the boiling point directly from the thermometer. For example, the barometer and thermometer Ziggah Porrah Zue stood 28.08 and 86°.

The boiling point of 28.06 (see Tables) is . . . . 208° Fah.
From Table I. for 208° height . . . . 2049 feet.
Proportional part of 0° 8′, deduct 408

$$\frac{}{1641}$$

Multiplier from Table II. for 86° 1112

Approximate height required . . . . 1824 feet.

The number of longitudes would have been greater, had it not been for the difficulty of reading off the limb of the sextant at night.

On the 14th of February, 1868, I embarked the effects of the expedition in a large canoe, loaned me by Dr. C. B. Dunbar for the purpose. We reached Virginia, on the St. Paul's, at six o'clock p. m. The next morning we started for Vannswah, a Dey village, four and a half miles in the rear of Virginia. This village was once occupied wholly by the Deys, but their power is fast waning, and more than half the village is now in the hands of Mandingo traders from Boporu.

Here it was that I had made a previous arrangement for the conduct of the expedition, with a learned Mandingo, Kaifal Kanda, who had lately arrived from his native town Billelah, a place near to, and scarcely second in importance to Musardu itself.

I was detained here three weeks waiting for him to to arrange our departure. In the mean time all my carriers, who were Kroomen, deserted me, with the exception of their head-man, Ben; being frightened by what the Dey people told them of the dangers of the road. Kaifal at first proposed to send me direct to Boporu; but my friends at Monrovia were so apprehensive that I should not be able to pass through that country, that I refused to go to Boporu. Subsequent events proved that their apprehensions were not entirely unfounded.

Boporu, though the most direct route, or the route most usually traveled, is also the place where the strongest opposition is offered to any one wishing to pass through. It is the place where the policy of non-intercourse originated Its policy and power dominate over the surrounding regions.

It was upon my refusal to go to Boporu that Kaifal sent me to Bessa's town, which is situated forty miles west of Boporu. And though it is somewhat independent of the authority of Momoru Son, the king of Boporu, the same practice prevails with respect to prohibiting all penetration into the interior.

Before setting out on this expedition, I made every effort to join another civilized person with me ; but the undertaking was considered of too dangerous a character. I tried to prevail on some of the young men, who had but little else to do at the time; but was so entirely unsuccessful, that I fear their reputation for enterprise and hardihood must suffer when I relate how they preferred the safe, soft, grassy streets of Monrovia to an expedition into the heart of their country, simply because it was said to be perilous. I thereafter received other discouragements, from such a quarter and of such a character that I must forbear to mention them.

Many stories were rife of the unsettled state of the country : that the roads between us and the interior tribes were infested by banditti, and that war was raging between interior tribes themselves ; that between all these jarring forces, it was impossible for the expedition to survive forty miles And this was the opinion of those who were in a condition to be the best informed. But as the expedition was pushed on in the very localities where these difficulties were said to exist, it was found that there were disturbances, but not of a characer to entirely prohibit our progress.

The practice of exaggerating every petty affair into the proportions of a universal war, is used for a purpose ; being often an artifice to produce general consternation, out of which the more knowing may cull every advantage for themselves.

Besides, it is the policy of our intervening tribes to get up scare-crow reports, to prevent intercourse between the interior and Liberia. Nothing is more dreaded, and especially by the Boporu Mandingoes, than the penetration of the interior by the Liberians. There is, therefore, a complete line of obstruction, extending east and west, in the rear of Montserrado county, which hinders or inconveniences trade. ˙ It deserves the immediate action of government, in order that the interior trade may be completely unfettered from such annoyances.

It is along this line that the Boporu Mandingoes and others are determined to be the "go-betweens" to the inland trade and Liberian enterprise. They it is who are chiefly engaged in making beef scarce, and country cloths small ; who trammel and clog the Boozie and Barline trade.

On the 6th of March, having hired eighteen Congoes, to supply the place of the Kroomen who had deserted me, we started from Vannswah for Bessa's town, under the conduct of two of Kaifal's young men. Bessa's town was the place pitched upon as our starting-point for Musardu, since I had refused to go to Boporu.

Passing, as rapidly as our burdens would permit, the towns of Vyrmore, Sne, Moah, Weta, and Bambu, we reached Manneenah on Thursday, the 12th of March. We had been traveling in a north-eastern direction; halting here, we saw a large mountain, north-east by east, behind which Boporu is said to lie. We had now to change our course to westward, in order to go to Bessa's town. All the towns and villages through which we had passed, except Weta, Bambu, and Maneenah, belong to the Deys. This tribe was once numerous and powerful, but is now scatteringly sprinkled in small and unimportant villages over the face of the country. They have a relic of their old antipathy against Liberians. Slave-trade, war, and their absorption into other tribes have nearly obliterated every thing that distinguished them as a tribe. Old Gatumba's town, both in appearance and hos-pitality, is the only redeeming feature in this part of the country.

In this region leopards are numerous, and sometimes dangerous. The female leopard is particularly dangerous when she has the care of her young. It is said that leopards never attack first, and will always shun you whenever they can do so   This rule, like many others, has some exceptions, and sometimes some very fatal ones. A female leopard having her cub with her met a man in a sudden turn of the road; she flew at him, and came nigh breaking the rule entirely as to him, but for the strength of his lungs and the speed of his legs, all of which had to be brought into desperate requisition.

At Weta's town an enormous leopard was shot by an old man. As soon as he saw the mammoth cat, he was taken with the trembles; but, remembering that it was only the matter of a few moments which should have the first chance for life, he leveled his piece at the head of the crouching animal, and in an instant had the satisfaction to see the object of his fears was stretched helpless on the earth.

This trophy of the old man's prowess was borne home in triumph, and divided into many parcels. The chine-bone is considered the bone of contention; and, as soon as it is severed from the rest, it is thrown high in the air, in order that when it comes to the ground—

"Those may take who have the power,
And those may keep who can."

A general scramble ensues, in which it is clearly proved that a part is greater than the whole ; for the chine-bone can produce a greater row, and a bigger fighter, than if the whole animal, instinct with its living ferocity, had jumped plump into the middle of the crowd.

The physical features of the country are roughened by hills, val- leys, and small plains; and similar inequalities of surface prevail to what may be seen in the rear of Clay Ashland ; indeed, the Clay Ashland hills are a part of them, and must have been produced by the same physical causes.

These hills grow bolder and more conspicuous in outline as we ad- vance in the interior. Sometimes linked together by gentle depres- sions, and sometimes entirely detached from each other, they form no definite range ; rising and running toward every point of the com- pass ; they present all the varieties of figure and direction that hills can assume.

Their composition, so far as could be discerned from their surface, was the ordinary vegetable mould, with boulders of iron ore, granite, white quartz, and a mixed detritus from these various rocks, charged in many places with thin-leaved mica, similar to that which is seen in the Clay Ashland hills.

Before we reached the margin of the Boporu, or Boatswain coun- try, we passed through long and almost unbroken strips of forests, upon a road partaking of the uneven character of the country, and strewn for miles with sharp pebbles and vitreous quartz, rendering travel painful enough to the unshodden pedestrian. Huge boulders of granite were dispensed here and there, relieving the gloom and monotony of large, shady forest trees. This region is intersected with numerous streams flowing over sandy bottoms or granite beds, with a temperature of 58°, 60°, and 62° Fahrenheit.

On Saturday, the 13th of March, we left Manneenah; and after traveling forty miles westward, we reached Bessa's town, at 6 P. M.

Bessa's town is in latitude 7° 3′ 19″, in the western portion of the Golah country. It is elevated about four hundred and eighty feet above the level of the sea. This town is located in a small, irregular plain, studded with palm trees, and hedged in by hills in nearly every direction. It is strongly fortified with a double barricade of large wooden stakes; in the space between each barricade sharp-pointed stakes, four feet long, are set obliquely in the ground, crossing each other; this is to prevent the defenses from being scaled. The town is of an oval form ; the north and the south points resting on the edge of swamps; the east and west points, which are the points of access, are flanked with a strong quadrilateral stockade, with four intervening gates between the outside gate and the town itself. There are guard-houses to each of these gates, and people constantly in them night and day. To a force without artillery this town would give some trouble. It contains about three hundred and fifty clay dwellings, of various sizes, and between eight hundred and one thousand inhabitants, who may be regarded as the permanent population. Of the transient traders and visitors it would be difficult to form any estimate. The houses are huddled together in a close and most uncomfortable proximity ; in some parts of the town scarcely two persons can walk abreast. In matters of cleanliness and health, King Bessa can not be said to have seriously consulted the interests of his people.

Bessa himself is a personage well known to one of our best citizens, Mr. Gabriel Moore. He is of Mandingo extraction. I regret, however, to say that he is deplorably wanting in that sedateness and religious cast of feeling which usually forms the distinguishing characteristic of that tribe.

I was informed that he had purchased a dispensation from the rigid observances of that creed from some of the Mandingo priests, by paying a large amount of money. This license to do evil so affected our journey to Musardu, that it came nearly breaking up the expedition altogether.

It was on a Friday we arrived in this town—a day said to be always inauspicious. We introduced ourselves as being sent to him by one of his own countrymen, Kaifal Kanda, a Mandingo, living at Vannswah, with whom we were going to Musardu.

He affected to listen with great attention ; spoke of the commotions of the interior, which, as he said, was a great obstacle and hinderance to all traveling just at that time. He also informed me that he would have to consult the other kings behind him before allowing me to pass ; and he kept on creating difficulty after difficulty, all reasonable and fair enough in argument, but pointblank lies in fact. He had no consulting to do ; for he was at that time at variance with the principal neighboring chiefs.

I was not pleased with my first audience. yet I was induced to make Bessa the following presents: three bars of tobacco, one double barrelled pistol, one large brass kettle, one piece of fancy handker-

Map of Liberia, showing journey to Musardu and return to Boporu.

This is a very imperfect map of Liberia, but it answers our purpose inasmuch as it plainly indicates the journey to Musardu. Since the printing of this map the settlements have extended 40 miles up the St. Paul instead of 20 as here stated. Harper is the most southerly point and Manna River near Bessa town the most northern. The length of the sea coast between these two points is 504 miles.

chiefs, and one keg of powder. This gift was received with satisfaction, but it was hinted that the king was anxious to trade with me for the rest of my money. I had, therefore, to distinctly state that I did not wish to trade, as that would prevent me from accomplishing the object for which I had come, namely, to go to Musardu.

Bessa now began to show how much he disrelished the idea of my passing through his country, and carrying so much money ' behind him," as he expressed it. He offered me his fat bullocks, country cloths, palm oil, ivory, etc., but I steadily refused to trade. Finding me inexorable in that respect he began to grumble about the "dash," or gifts, I had made him. Some mischievous persons had told him that the gifts were insignificant to what it was the custom of Liberians to "dash," or present, kings; and Jollah, my interpreter, had some difficulty to persuade the king to the contrary; besides, he had his own reasons for remaining so incredulous

I had now struck the line of obstruction at this point. It was upon my refusal to go to Boporu that Kaifal had sent me to Bessa's town. Bessa, in carrying out this policy of non-intercourse with the interior, which is a standing, well-known, and agreed-upon thing throughout the whole country, now commenced a series of annoyances, his people acting in concert with him He began with my Congoes. Every means that language and signs could produce was used to frighten and discourage them. They were told of the wars in the path. He also showed some Boozies whom he had in his town, whose faces were disfigured with hideous tattoo marks, and whose front teeth were filed sharp and pointed, for the purpose of eating people; their long bows and poisoned arrows; their broad knives and crooked iron hooks, with which they caught and hewed to pieces those whom they pursued. But what more alarmed my Congoes than anything else, was the prospect of being eaten by the Boozies. Bessa, to make this part more vividly horrible, had brought into our presence several of his man-eaters, who were said to delight in that business. He then brought in his war drums, the heads of which were the skins of human beings, well tanned and corded down. while a dozen grinning human jaw-bones were dangling and rattling against each other with a noise that reminded my Congoes that their jaw-bones too might perform a similar office on some country war-drum. It was by such means that Bessa entirely succeeded in disorganizing the whole expedition. He gave the Congoes plainly to understand that they had better not hazard their lives in attempting to follow me to Musardu.

My carriers, who had hitherto shown willingness and obedience, now began openly to disobey my orders; and my difficulty was greatly increased from the fact that I had not been able to get a single civilized person to accompany me. I had no one, in consequence, to confer with, or to assist me in watching the movements of my mutinous Congoes. It soon became evident that there was an understanding between my Congoes and Bessa, and that all hands were conspiring together against me. Several times I had detected Bessa and the Congoes in secret consultation. I guessed at once the villainy hatching. I tried every means to induce the Congoes to disregard the idle tales that were told them by Bessa and his people; but neither advice, persuasion, nor the offer of donations above their pay could overcome the impression that had been made upon their minds respecting the dangers of the route. Big Ben, the Krooman, kept himself aloof from the plots of the Congoes, yet he was in favor of returning to Monrovia; and he made my ears ring with, "Spose we no find good path; we go back now." The Congoes began to hold secret meetings by themselves, and to talk in a low, muttering tone. Matters were now brewing to some mischievous point; but what their resolves were, I could never learn. With my Congoes in open rupture, Bessa himself drunk, avaricious, and conspiring, I had now to exercise thhe greatest vigilance.

One night, exasperated at their mutinous language and conduct, we came to a collision, in which all of us had recourse to our arms, and but for the immediate interference of the town people, things would have certainly ended seriously. I should have been riddled with their balls, there being fifteen of them. King Bessa, attended by some of his people, came to allay the disturbance. He could not have been furnished with a better opportunity of seemingly protecting me from the very mischiefs he had secretly instigated. He reproved the Congoes, and imposed a fine for breaking the peace—a gun and a piece of handkerchief being the cost of court. He never used his authority to enforce obedience on the part of the Congoes, which he could have easily done. No; he affected a neutral course, which had many by-paths to his own interest, and through which he managed to transfer many a bar of my tobacco into his own hands.

Much of Bessa's conduct arose from the defiant and refractory behavior of Prince Manna toward the government. The moral effect of this man's conduct has been anything but beneficial to Liberia.

Bessa was continually referring, with pride, to a man who could defy the government with impunity. Unless the government shows energy and control, it will always be difficult to visit these parts—almost within the territorial limits of Liberia—for any purpose whatever. The fact was but too plainly humiliating, that we had lost *prestige* and respect. The policy of too much moderation and forbearance is often abused or misunderstood by warlike barbarians, whose swords are an appendage of their daily apparel.

Bessa now, in an advisory manner, repeated over and over again the difficulties of the route, adding to it the determination of my Congo carriers themselves not to go any further. To this he joined a series of petty annoyances—sometimes coming himself, and sometimes sending for me, to talk palavers. Then he would complain that the Congoes endangered the lives of his people by their hunting; that they would likely set his town on fire by their smoking-pipe, though his own people indulged in this thing not only to a greater degree, but solely through my liberality. But what exasperated me most was his practice of eavesdropping; his boys and people were continually lurking to hear what was said in my house. I was always expected to conclude his royal visits—which were frequent, and which he gave me to understand were condescensions on his part—with large bars of my tobacco.

Bessa is naturally avaricious. This vice was unfortunately worked up to its worst resource; he drank night and day, until he had sufficiently steamed himself up to the courage for downright robbery. Drunk he gets every day; and after the first two or three hours of excess are over, he finally sobers down to that degree at which his avarice is greatest, and his regard for other's rights least. There he remains.

His couch, upon which he reclines, and which is at once his bed and his chair of state, he never quits, but for a drunken carousal in the midst of his women. This bed is stacked head and foot with loaded muskets, huge horse-pistols rusty swords and spears, while sundry daggers, with their points stuck in the ground, are ready at hand "for the occasion sudden." He seems to live in perpetual dread of assassination. His people never come in his presence but in an obsequious stoop, and they never recover an erect posture until they are out of his presence. But when the women came then you might expect to see humanity go on all fours. It was difficult to know the height of some of the women on account of their servility.

Bessa is engaged in the slave-trade. Passing one morning through his town I saw a slave with his right hand tied up to his neck, and fifty sticks of salt fastened to his back, about to be sent into the interior to be exchanged for a bullock. Six slaves, chained together, worked on his farms. He has numerous other slaves, but they were better treated.

I will not relate all the circumstances of his lashing an old slave until his cries drew the tears of all who stood by, nor his stamping in the breast of one of his slaves until death ensued, on account of some slight offense. His enormities are too many to recount them all, and would only weary the reader with what they know must be his habits, from what I have already said of him. He regretted to me the interference of the Liberians with the foreign slave trade.

It was now the beginning of April, and I had not been able to proceed upon my journey. My Congo carriers refused to go any further. Kaifal, the Mandingo, still remained at Vannswah. I therefore tried to induce Bessa to hire me some of his people. I offered to pay him liberally if he would honestly engage in sending me forward. He accepted the offer, and received an amount of $66.40 in goods. He gave me four persons, to act as interpreters and guides; but I had no one to carry luggage, and he took good care that no one should be hired for that purpose He was continually telling me that my money "no got feet this time."

If I could have relied on my Congoes, I would have gone on despite Bessa's attempts to prevent me; but their defection paralyzed all movement forward. I could bethink myself of no other resource than to return to Vannswah in quest of Kaifal. Not having any one in whom I could repose confidence enough to place my effects in their care until I returned from Vannswah, I had to run the risk of placing them in the hands of the king. On the 5th of April, 1868, taking two of my Congoes with me, I came to Boporu. There I met Seymoru Syyo, Kaifal's relation, a tall, fine-looking Mandingo, but whose very black countenance wore a still blacker cloud of displeasure because I had not come to him direct, instead of going to Bessa. He scarcely deigned to look at me, especially as I was in no decent plight, having undertaken the journey barefoot, in order to cross the streams more readily. He at length gave me to understand that, so far as Kaifal's going to Musardu was concerned, it depended entirely upon his (Seymoru Syyo's) pleasure, muttered something about the war at Musardu; counted his beads and then strode off toward the mosque where they had just been summoned to prayer.

On the 6th of April, 1868, I started from Boporu, and arrived at Vannswan on the 9th. Kaifal affected regret at having caused me so much delay, telling me that it was owing to his preparation to get ready that he was detained so long. He now promised to march immediately. This he made a show of doing by sending his women and scholars forward, telling me to go on with them, while he should remain behind to pray for our success. I consented; but he managed to lag behind so long, that I never saw him again until May 8th, after I had left Bessa's and come to Boporu.

I now went back to Bessa's town, persuaded that Kaifal would soon follow. As soon as I arrived at Bessa's, Ben, the Krooman, informed me that the Congoes had tried to induce the king to send them home, telling him that he might keep all my goods if he would only permit them to go home. I went straight to the king, and requested him to deliver to me my boxes; he at once hesitated, and I could scarcely get him to consent to let me have the box containing my clothes. After much contention and wrangling, he delivered up all the boxes, retaining the powder and guns. He then declared that I must pay him for all the Congoes I had placed in his hands; that I must pay him a piece of cloth and a gun for each one of them, as well as for feeding them while I was gone to Vannswah. He then made some other frivolous demands, which he deemed necessary to justify the robbery he was about to commit.

To make the matter worse, the Congoes themselves now began to gather round me like little children. begging me to sacrifice all my goods, if it were necessary, to save them "Daddy, no lose we this country, no lose we," was their continual whine. All spirit for a manly resistance had fled; nothing but the most abject cowardice prevailed. Before I started on the journey, I had thoroughly armed these Congoes; but the only use they had made of their arms was to resist my authority. Now a peculiar danger stared them in the face— they had not even courage enough to save themselves from slavery.

I refused to comply with the demands of the king to pay the boys. I became exasperated; but I was jammed between the power of the king and the cowardice and unfaithfulness of the Congoes. The king's Boozies, who walked the town with their broad knives to fight,

and their teeth filed sharp to eat their enemies, confirmed the pol-
troonery of the Congoes as a standing axd immutable fact.

The king advised the Congoes to talk to me, telling them, "Your
daddy has got the heart of an elephant; you had better talk to
him." They attempted to talk to me; but I was too much angered
at their cowardice and his robbery to listen to any thing. The king
extorted $130; Ben, the Krooman, and Louis, a Congo, negotiating
the business. I refused to have any thing to do with it. After he
had taken this amount, Ben and Louis begged him to bè satisfied.
He told them that he would refer the matter to his women; if they
consented, he would rest satisfied. This female assembly was consulted, and from the subsequent conduct of the king, they must
have resolved that I should pay doubly. The extortions were renewed
to an amount of $25. This occurred on Friday and Saturday, the
23rd and 24th of April.

The next day I was somewhat able to command my feelings. I
resolved to go to Bǫporu. Nothing was more contrary to Bessa's
wishes. He now tried his best to induce me to go on my journey
through his country. He declared that unless the Congoes wanted to
lose their heads, they should go along with me. He was willing to furnish guides and interpreters. But my resolution was taken; I was
determined to go to Boporu; no blandishments nor hollow profes-
sions of friendship could lead me to trust him after what I had just
experienced at his hands. As he had been visited by some suspicious
persons, who even counted the number of my Congo warriors, it
might have been agreed on to finish with murder what had been
begun by robbery. We were allowed to depart without further annoyance. The Congoes were overjoyed; for they were sure I was returning home. Bessa even sent six stalwart slaves to carry me, in order
that my feelings might be soothed into some kind of forbearance
toward him; for he now began to fear that I might bring him to
account, though it seemed he was willimg to run the risk rather than
restore the goods. I availed myself of the service of his carriers;
bui I left the king with the bitter intention to do him all the injury I
could as soon as opportunity presented itself.

I arrived at Boporu on the 25th of April, 1868. Kaifal had not
yet come, and did not arrive until three days afterward. He now
appeared indignant at Bessa's conduct, and affected the greatest dili.
gence for our setting out immediately for Musardu. But first, he

would go to Bessa and influence him to restore what he had unjustly taken from me. He induced me to make considerable presents to his friend and relation, Seymoru Syyo, helping himself also in a manner which nothing but my great anxiety for him to hasten our journey would have allowed me to permit.

Before he went to Bessa's, the principal Mandingoes in the town, Kaifal, and myself, held a council, in which they strove to induce me to return to Bessa's with Kaifal; but I utterly refused. I would talk of nothing but soldiers, cannon, the burning of Bessa's town, and other furious things; which so alarmed the Mandingoes, that they begged me not to write to Monrovia about the matter until Kaifal had gone and tried to get the money. In this council, the Mandingoes reminded me that, as the Liberians and Mandingoes were one and the same people, I ought not to act with too great a severity; but I was not inclined to make common stock of my goods on account of that identity, and in a very impatient and unreasonable manner I gave them to understand that all their relationship to me depended solely on the restoration of my goods. If they failed in that, I was prepared to ignore all ties. I was in no humor for cant about kindred.; I wanted my money; my feelings were sore at my disappointments and losses.

The expedition was deemed to have fallen in pieces. My interpreter, Jollah, also commenced to show signs of desertion and treachery. I had always suspected him with being implicated in Bessa's villainy; I was soon to discover that he had not been entirely ignorant nor innocent with respect to Bessa's designs. His connivance, or rather the assistance he gave Bessa, was so glaring, that the Mandingoes at Boporu did not fail to upbraid him with it. In his conversation, he plainly showed that he had gone over to Bessa's interest, though he still continued to follow my boxes. The Mandingoes contemptuously asked him in whose service he was, whether mine or Bessa's? Bessa, it seemed, had promised him largely if he (Jollah) assisted him successfully in his villainy. Jollah's crooked ways were such that I could no longer retain his services. Interpreters began to prove a dangerous attachment to the expedition. Owing to Jollah's double-dealing, I was obliged to have recourse to a Veyman to act as interpreter; and right in the middle of an important conversation which I was holding with Seymoru Syyo, this man suffered himself to be taken so ill as to become speechless, and he could only be induced to recover by the promise of a large (dash) present.

Kaifal, it seemed, had greatly offended Seymoru Syyo by sending me to Bessa's instead of sending me direct to Boporu; but, as I have before shown, it was not Kaifal's fault that I did not go directly to Boporu. However, the fault was imputed to him, and as he could only regain the favor of Seymoru by gifts, it was thought no more than right that I should bestow them, as it was through my persistence in refusing to go to Boporu that he had got into the difficulty with Seymoru. As soon as my boxes arrived at Boporu, Seymoru altered his demeanor toward me. His dark and grumbling countenance immediately changed into a smiling intimacy and friendship. He would fain have posted me on wings to Musardu.

Though Boporu is the capital of the Boatswain or Condo country, and the usual residence of the king, Momoru Son, the king was at this time residing at a large town called Totoquella, eight miles northeast of Boporu.

As soon as Kaifal started for Bessa's town, I resolved to pay my respects to King Momoru. I arrived at Totoquella on May 7th, 1868. I was kindly received, and at once stated to the king that I would have been to see him much sooner, but that I was a stranger in his country, and had supposed that he resided at his reputed capital, Boporu; that when I came to that town, I was informed that he had gone elsewhere. He replied that he was accustomed to divide his time between the two towns; sometimes residing at Boporu and sometimes staying at Totoquella. I then informed him of the object of my visit; and had to frame such an account of my former proceedings as to show that it had always been my intention to come to his country, but that I had been thwarted by many untoward circumstances. And true it was that I would have preferred, at the first, going direct to Boporu, had it not been for the reasons already stated.

Circumstances now forced me in that direction, and I addressed myself to the task of repairing the failures or misfortunes into which the expedition had fallen. The king was intelligent and communicative. He was, however, chagrined that the government—the new administration of which had just come into power—had not taken any notice of him, and sent him a (book) paper, expressive of its good feelings toward him, as had been the custom of all incoming administrations. He was always referring to a treaty that had been made between him and President Benson, during the incumbency of the latter. I had, therefore, to console him with the notion that, as soon as the administration had got fairly into operation, it would not fail to draw up an instrument similar to what President Benson had given him; as well as to make such other arrangement as would satisfy his utmost wishes. The king informed me that he was at that moment trying to stop a war between the Boozies and Barlines, two interior tribes; that he had, in order to promote that purpose, sent five hundred sticks of salt into the Barline country, and the same amount to the Boozies; that he had instructed his messengers to use every argument to incline the parties to peace; that the war was not only hurtful to themselves, but that it damaged him by interrupting all intercourse between his country and theirs, and even with the natives whose country lay behind them. He had sent, therefore, to beg both parties to desist; but if neither would listen, he intended to indemnify himself for such losses as he sustained by their feuds. by seizing persons and property belonging to them in his country. If only one party was willing to comply with his requests, he intended to assist that side with his own military forces.

Thus I had to endure the spectacle of a barbarian king practicing a policy which all intelligent and enterprising persons must think ought to be practiced by the republic itself. No one suspects that we leave to an untutored barbarian the quieting and settling of interior difficulties, while we remain ignorant of their very existence.

Every one would suppose that to a source to which we look for a great part of our interior trade, such as country cloths, and bullocks, and ivory, a rational solicitude, at least. would be shown that it be not interrupted or broken off. Yet it is a fact that this royal barbarian, without revenue and without any of the resources to which we pretend, by following the policy of interfering in all interior concerns, is better known and has greater influence from Boporu to Musardu, and even beyond, than the civilized Republic of Liberia; and this is done by sending a few sticks of salt, accompanied by a friendly request or a threatening mandate.

Salt in the settling of difficulties, has a peculiar propriety—it is a sign of peace as well as a commodity of value for traffic. If it was the policy of the government to interfere in these concerns, a hogshead of salt might pacify the whole country from Boporu to Barline. The king had also interfered in a matter between the Boozies themselves, in which it seemed that one of their chiefs, faithless to the common interest, had clandestinely given assistance to the Barlines against his own countrymen. This treachery being discovered, he had been seized and confined—or put in stick, as they call it. This mode of confinement consists in having the ankle of the right foot bound securely to a heavy log, four or five feet long, by means of an iron band driven deep into the wood.

The father of this recreant chief, before his death, had placed his children under King Momoru's protection. The king was therefore solicitous that this indiscretion should not cost the young prince his liberty, and perhaps his head ; of the former of which he had already been deprived, and the latter was being seriously discussed among the Boozie chiefs. In this affair the king desired that, as I would have to pass through that country, he wished me to assist in pleading for the young man. I pledged my best efforts.

There was also a difficulty between the king and the Boondee people, who live north-west of Boporu. These people hold a nominal fealty to King Momoru, and even this they are slack or remiss in acknowledging.

The king now chose to remove his court from Totoquella to Boporu. None was more eager for this change than myself ; for it carried his person and influence just where I wished to make use of them. He left the town May 10th, 1868, accompanied by his courtiers, warriors, women, servants, and musicians of the last of which there were two kinds : those who performed on horns and drums, and those who sang the praises of the king, timing their music with a sort of iron cymbal, one part being fitted to the thumb of the left hand and beaten with a piece of iron by the right.

When the king and his retinue had passed the outer gates of the barricade, a Mandingo priest came out and pronounced a benediction on the royal departure. As soon as this was over, we started ; the king walking all the way : he had but to say the word, and they would have carried him. We were preceded by the singing men, who, with the clang of their iron cymbals and their vociferous vocalisms, nearly deafened me. After two or three hours spent in traveling, halting, singing, firing muskets, and all sorts of noisy demonstrations, we came to Boporu. The king entered the town and went directly to his own residence. Everybody came to do homage and welcome his arrival. But nothing appeared more respectful than the Mandingo priests, who came in a body, habited in their white and scarlet robes;

tall, dignified black men, with countenances solemn and intelligent. It is remarkable how orderly and sociable these gatherings upon such occasions conduct themselves. Nothing of the rowdyism and clamor for which communities highly civilized are sometimes notorious. The day was concluded with dancing, feasting, and warlike exercises. The next day beheld everything settled down into its usual routine. I was now to discover the character of Kaifal in its true light. He had always affected piety and uprightness; nothing very material had occurred to alter my opinion. To be sure, he had lately shown intense craving for my large silver spoon, yet I was inclined to be charitable to this human weakness. He went to Bessa's, solemnly assuring me that he would be gone but two or three days; he staid three weeks, which caused my patience, and confidence, too, to grow less. I dispatched two of my boys after him. Upon the return of my messengers, I was informed that he had been generously entertained by Bessa, that a sheep had been slain, and other good offices done for him. I became alarmed lest such friendly cheer would lessen his zeal to recover my goods. But when I was further informed that Kaifal had been engaged in practicing certain rites, such as the interment of beef bones bound round with transcripts from the Koran, which was to be efficacious for Bessa in peace or war, I immediately understood this last act to be directed against myself. I therefore lost no time in ingratiating myself with the king. And there was scarcely anything I had to propose that was not favorably entertained and facilitated. I had strengthened my influence by gifts, as well as by the great amusement my stereoscope afforded him. I had thoroughly instructed him in the purposes of my mission, and showed him how discreditable it would be to his name and his honor if anything should befall me and my effects within the precincts of his dominions, so that I should not be able to carry out the wishes of the promoters of the expedition. In this part of my affairs I was particularly blessed by Providence in getting in my interest a near relation of the king's. He was a Golah man by the civilized name of Chancelor. He had long resided both at Monrovia and Cape Palmas with one of the best citizens, Dr. S. F. McGill, and could speak English fluently, besides several native tongues. He adhered with unflagging zeal to my interest, and never ceased importuning his royal kinsman night and day respecting my affairs. He was of mild disposition, full of encouragement and sympathy; having nothing to

contradict the universal benevolence of his person and character
except a huge, antiquated horse-pistol, without which he was never
seen, and which became a subject of merriment, as being a burden
without a benefit, perfectly innocent in all things except its weight.
I had now determined to use all my influence against Kaifal and Bessa. I had been robbed of one part of my goods by the one, and
inveigled out of another part by the other. The purposes of the
expedition had been baffled, though I had striven to the utmost to
accomplish them.

Momoru might be avaricious, but his avarice was a virtue to Bessa's
rapacity and Kaifal's unprincipled dealings. If the king wished me
to give him anything, his requests were always ac ompanied with
politeness and desert, arising from the prospect of his facilitating my
journey to Musardu. I made a formal complaint against Kaifal and
Bessa, presenting the king a written list of all the goods they had un-
fairly gotten from me. He convened the leading Mandingoes of the
town and the principal chiefs. The king himself opened this grand
palaver, declaring ''that owing to the acts of some of the Mandingoes,
many things had been said by the Liberians tending to lessen his
character. Whenever the Liberians lost their money by trade or
otherwise, he had always to bear the brunt of their dishonest actions
and to suffer all kinds of disparagement of character.'' Nor did he
neglect to cite the instances, mentioning as a particular case that of
John B. Jordan, who had traded in that country and lost considerable
amounts; and then he went on in detail, until he became angered.
The Mandingoes found it necessary to appease him by all sorts of
condescension; even the singing men were called in. It was necessary to adjourn, that the royal displeasure might cool off.

The next day the business was resumed. It is the custom for every
body taking part in a (palaver) discussion, to deliver his argument or
opinion walking up and down in the presence of his audience with a
spear in his hands.

This mode was observed by all the chiefs who spoke on this occasion. Many of them delivered themselves with such spirit and sense
as to draw the frequent acclamations of their hearers. They declared
that they not only ought to be careful about provoking the Americans
against them ; but, as the money was for the purpose of (dashing)
presenting the chiefs through whose country I might pass, I ought
to be allowed to give it to whom I wished ; and that none ought to

accept it unless they were willing to accept the conditions of the gift also.

For the conduct of Bessa and Kaifal, the Mandingoes at Boporu seemed to have been held as sureties; certainly not by their own will or consent, but by virtue of their being most conveniently at hand for any purpose of indemnification that might arise. Kaifal, who was still at Bessa's town, was summoned to appear. Bessa was ordered to refund every article according to the list.

The messenger charged with this business went to Bessa's in the most formal manner, being in complete war dress It was, therefore, understood that there was to be no trifling.

Things began now to conspire in my favor.

Just about this time a young man by the name of Sanders Washington, from the settlement of Virginia, went to Bessa's town for the purpose of trading. Here he learned what had happened between Bessa and myself. He at once advised Bessa to restore the money before the consequences became serious. Bessa, becoming more sober than was usual with him, commenced to apprehend a severe chastising from the government, and right upon the heels of what was to be feared from the Americans came Momoru's no less dreaded demands.

Bessa quickly gave up the things to Mr. Sanders Washington, and consoled himself in a drunken spree. Mr. Washington immediately sent the things to Boporu.

Kaifal now made his appearance. It was the 28th of May, 1868. He came before the king and council dressed in a dark-blue tobe; a red cap bordered with a white band, the badge of his sacerdotal order, on his head; sandals on his feet; his prayer-beads in his hands; his face and faculties prepared for the worst. He was ordered to account for the manner he had conducted my affai s. He commenced defending himself by declaring that what had happened to me was the result of my own obstinacy; for when he wished to send me directly to Boporu, I had insisted on going elsewhere. He further said that if I could have passed through the country anywhere else, they would have never seen my face at Boporu; which was indeed true. He caused disagreeable questions to be put to me respecting that mat ter: this was his only advantage, and he clung to it. He declared that I had absolutely refused to go to Boporu and that I had maligned the king, and that I had gone to Bessa's, where my indiscretion had got me into trouble and made me lose my money; that Bessa had acted in all things honestly.

His argument was partly true and partly false. All he averred respecting Boporu was indeed true ; but borrowing the courage which the truth about Boporu gave him, his assertions about Bessa's conduct were bold and barefaced lies. I replied that it was solely upon his advice that I had gone to Bessa's; that as to my coming to Boporu, he plainly saw I was there, and that without consulting him.

He dwelt incessantly on my refusal to go to Boporu, and more than once it was convenient for me to rid myself of his vexing questions by placing the whole blame upon his interpreter.

We now came to that part in which he had taken my money and gone off to Bessa's, where he had staid so long that it became necessary to send for |him. Being questioned why he had done so, his self-possession entirely forsook him, and though he referred the matter to a rapid manipulation of his beads, it brought him no relief. He told them over and over, but they failed to enlighten his mind so as to furnish prompt replies and ready answers. He finally stammered out something about his waiting for the new moon. He had not regarded that luminary when he was getting the goods.

He was made to restore according to the list.

I was now in possession of all my goods again, with the prospect of being able to prosecute the exploration with success.

I was also in a better state of mind to attend to my affairs in that respect, though, as I had all along apprehended, the season for comfortable traveling, and especially for making astronomical observations, had nearly passed ; indeed, upon every attempt at an observation, clouds and vapor made it a dfficult and uncertain matter.

Boporu, the capital of the Boatswain country, is in latitude 7° 45.08″. Its elevation above the level of the sea is about 560 feet. The barometer in the month of May and June, stands from 29.18 to 29.40 ; the thermometer ranges from 78 to 80 Fahrenheit. It is situated in a small plain near the foot of some high hills E N.E. of it. Very high hills rise on every side, with an elevation from 300 to 650 feet, coursing along in every direction some continuing three or four miles in length before their spurs come down into the valleys or plains. The soil of the plains is chiefly white and yellow clay ; but near the base of the hills, it is generally mixed with the detritus of granite and other rocks washed down in the rainy season from their sides. Granite boulders of various sizes are found on the sides and tops of these hills, and, unlike the granite of our cape, which is of a

fine, dark flinty appearance, present many grades of tint and texture.
A large piece of this granitic gneiss forms a part of the grave of King
Boatswain, the present kings's father, broken in such a way as to
show the red, white, and gray in beautiful contrast. A little art
might have rendered it more worthy to mark so mighty a grave.
Every tree, flower, and shrub of our cape repeats itself here, not
excepting the water-lilies seen in the creeks as you go to Junk, though
not in the same profusion.

At Totoquella, northeast of Boporu, and four hours' walk south-
east from the former, the St. Paul's River presents rugged and impas-
sable falls. Northwest of Totoquella are beds of specular iron ore,
which the natives break into fragments and use for shot.

The population of Boporu is of a mixed character, such as war,
commerce, and the domestic slave-trade are calculated to produce;
in consequence of which there are as many different languages spoken
as there are tribes: Vey, Golah Mambomah, Mandingo, Pessy,
Boozie, Boondee, and the Hurrah languages. The Vey language is
used for general communication. The extent and population of
these tribes are very variable elements. The population living in the
town may be set down at three thousand, but then there are many
outlying villages and hamlets; and considering these as the suburbs
of Boporu, they undoubtedly raise the population to ten thousand.
Many of the Mandingoes themselves, though they reside in the town
with their families, have villages of slaves and servants scattered in
every direction, wherever the purposes of agriculture invite or encour
age.

The Mandingoes possess strong moral influence. Scarcely anything
is undertaken without consulting their priests, whose prayers, blessings, and other rites are supposed to give a propitious turn to all the
affairs of peace and war. They are Mohammedans; but as the ruder
tribes do not addict themselves to the intellectual habits of the Mandingoes, it has been found necessary to adjust that faith to the necessities of the case; and to temper some of the mummeries of fetichism with the teachings of Islam. Yet are there to be found individuals who do not prostitute their faith, and who are more scrupulous
and sincere. It is believed by many persons that the Arabic learning
of our Mandingoes, in reading and writing from the Koran, is merely
mechanical, or a mere matter of memory.

Raifal took a small Arabic grammar given to me by Professor Blyden, and showed himself thoroughly versed in all the distinctions of person, gender, and number, etc., in the conjugation of a verb. However, all are not equally proficient in this respect.

They have a mosque at Boporu, where nothing enjoined by their religion is omitted. It is attended solely by the Mandingoes, none of the other tribes visiting it; not because they are prohibited, for the Mandingoes would make proselytes of them all if they could. It is sufficient for the "Kaffirs," (unbelievers,) as they are denominated by the Mandingoes, to buy the amulets, necklaces, and belts containing transcripts from the Koran sewed up in them, to be worn around the neck, arms, or waist as preservatives from the casualties of war, sickness, or ill luck in trade or love.

The Mandingoes are scrupulously attentive to their worship They regularly attend their services three times a day: five o'clock in the morning; three o'clock in the afternoon; and seven o'clock iu the evening.

In these services I was particularly attracted by the manner in which they chanted the cardinal article of their creed; and many a morning have I been reminded of my own duty, by their solemn musical voices reciting:

La il-la-ha il-al-la hu Ma-hamma-du ra-sul il-la-hi.

The Mandingoes living in the Boatswain country have many slaves. The slave population is supposed to treble the number of free persons. They are purchased chiefly from the Pessy, Boozie, and other tribes. Many are reduced to the condition of slaves, by being captured in war. Their chief labor is to perform the service of carriers for their masters in the trade of salt and country cloths carried between Boporu and Vannswah.

Inconveniences and troubles frequently arise from this kind of relationship. Sensible of their numbers and strength, the slaves sometime make a struggle for their liberty. In the latter part of 1866, at the death of Torsu, King Momoru's uncle it became necessary to settle some debts pertaining to Torsu's estate. His relatives, in order to pay off the claims, attempted to sell some of his slaves. These slaves were staying at a town called Musadalla's town, south-west of Boporu. The attempt was resisted; some blood was shed; and a general revolt took place, in which all the slaves in the town determined to defend each other to the last extremity. They took full possession of the town, renewed the barricades, seized upon whatever arms were at hand, and made such other preparations as greatly alarmed their masters. This rebellion had been long purposed on ; the death of Torsu and the attempt to sell some of their number, served as a favorable opportunity to achieve their freedom.

On the first outbreak King Momoru sent them word to return to their former obedience, assuring them that he would overlook all past offenses. But while they were deliberating as to what answer they should return, one of their women publicly harangued them against listening to any proposals for reconciliation ; that King Momoru only wished to induce them to submit, that he might the more easily punish them ; that if their hearts began to quail, they had better give their spears into the hands of the women.

This speech instantly determined them to stand fast in their first resolutions. Refusing all accommodation, they sought to strengthen their cause by purchasing the assistance of the Boondee people, who were at that time at variance with the people at Boporu. But the Boporu people had also managed, despite their difference with the Boondee people, to engage their services against the slaves. The Boondee war chief received the gifts of both parties ; and in two weeks' time repaid the poor slaves with treachery enough to chop off their heads

Arming himself and his people, he set out for Musadalla's town, and was admitted by his unsuspecting victims. After he had rested from his journey, and refreshed himself and his followers on their generosity, he proposed to review their numbers and their arms. Pretending to be earnestly enlisted in their affairs, he bade them lay their arms on the ground, or as we term it, "ground arms," that he might the better judge of their efficiency. The poor, credulous fools, by no means suspecting any perfidy, readily did as they were bid. At a given signal from the Boondee chief, his own people instantly drew their swords and bestrode the weapons of the poor slaves as they lay on the ground.

Thus disarmed, they were thus again enslaved, seized, bound, and led out of the gates to the town of their betrayer, who at once sent word to Momoru that he had caught the "slave dogs." He was rewarded, or rather he rewarded himself, by keeping all the women and children, sending to Momoru only the men and our heroine who, by her speech, had so greatly encouraged the matter. It was determined in council that the slaves should suffer the penalty of death.

On the morning of the execution they were demanded to say who were the chief instigators of the revolt; the poor creatures had but little to say. They were led out of the eastern gate, two hundred yards from which, and in the same direction stands a huge cotton tree (bombax)—the place of execution. They came down the path naked and in single file, with their hands bound behind them. As the first person came on, the executioner with his broad and gleaming knife ran to meet him, and with dexterous cruelty emasculated him; after allowing him to bleed and beg awhile, he was snatched down to the foot of the tree, his head hacked off and tossed into a ditch on one side of the road; while the yet quivering trunk was thrown into a cat fish pond hard by.

The woman was executed with circumstances shocking to humanity and decency. All the women in Boporu were compelled to go out and witness her fate.

But to the chief of this revolt it was reserved to be buried alive, heels up and head down, and a sharp stake, eight feet long, driven through his body level with the ground, and a tree planted over him. Their skulls now form a ghastly adornment to the eastern gate; and I have seen many persons go up to them and recognize an acquintance.

It seems to be the practice in every town where the water favors it to have catfish pools. 'The fish are not allowed to be disturbed; they are not only the consumers of the offal of the town, but from their shark-like and snappish manner, a more fearful office can well be suspected. They are from one to three feet long, and will lie with patience and expectation in one spot all day long, their backs raw with scars, which their own ferocity inflicts on each other in the fierce struggle for food.

Boporu has a small market, held in the north east suburbs of the town   The bartering is carried on solely by women. There is no established currency; the exchange takes place of one commodity for another, according to their mutual necessities. It is generally attended by one hundred and seventy-five to two hundred persons. The articles are palm-oil, rice, kaffee-seed, shallots—a small species of onion—meat, cotton stripes, tobacco, kola, earthern pots, etc   A great many country cloths are made at Boporu, every family having a small loom   They would economize both time and labor if they employ our large loom, instead of the narrow six inch loom they use.

I have no doubt they would do so, if any civilized person would interest himself to show them.

These people are very sensible of the superiority of every thing that comes from (Dru-kau) Monrovia, and they attempt to practice our civilization of themselves.

Just after the journey to Musardu was printed, the following letter was received from Rev. E W. BLYDEN, Professor in Liberia College:

MONROVIA, February 5, 1870.

REV. J B PINNEY:

DEAR SIR: I have just returned from a brief visit to the Boporu regions. Mr. W Winwood Reade, an English traveler, author of *South Africa*, accompanied me. Rev. O. W. Gibson, of the Episcopal Church anxious to respond to the urgent calls which are so loudly made for teachers from that quarter. sent out with me one of his candidates for orders to open a school in that country. The King, Momoru, was not at Boporu when we reached that town, but at Toto Coreh a fortified town ten miles on the east. We proceeded thither, where the king received us in fine style, and especially welcomed the teacher Two days after we arrived, on Friday, January 21st, he called his principal men together in a large open building in the town, and presented in their presence his own and his brother's children to form the nucleus of a school.

He exhorted the people on the importance of such establishments among them. He said that he himself having lived a little while at Monrovia, when a boy—sent thither by King Boatswain, his father, —had gained some insight into civilization, which had proved of so much advantage to him, and he only regretted that his knowledge was so exceedingly limited. He now felt grateful for the opportunity afforded him of introducing among the children of his country the advantage of book learning.

I then read a chapter from the Bible and prayed, after which I took down the names of the boys presented and gave them primers. They seemed delighted. After introducing to them the teacher — who m de a few remarks—and entreating them to be kind to him, I dismissed the assembly by permission of the king. That was a day long to be remembered by all who were present. To me it was a great and solemn privilege. Mr. Winwood Reade, who proclaims himself a free thinker, and who has not much faith in missions as re ligious agencies, could not resist the infl ence of the occasion. He drew up a paper giving his impressions of the country, etc., which he left with the king. I send you a copy herewith.

Mr. Gibson has assumed a great responsibility in opening a school at Toto-Coreh. I hope he will be sustained by his board. The Episcopalians are thus first in the field, but the field is large and needy.

Copy of a written statement made by Mr. W. Winwood Reade, and left with Momoru, Cing of the Condo country:

TOTO-KORIE, January 22, 1870.

I desire to state that having paid a visit to Momoru, resident in this town, he received me hospitably, and made me a handsome present when I left him

Momoru is evidently the most powerful king in the regions interior of Monrovia He possesses the road from Musardu and other inland states to the sea; the whole of their trade is therefore in his hands.

It is my opinion that the favor of this king should be cultivated, not only by the Liberian government but also by missionaries, travelers and foreign merchants.

Momoru having received some education in Liberia, has much larger views than most native chiefs. On the present ocasion a school having been established under the auspices of Professor Blyden, of Liberia College, he has shown a most laudable desire to further the education of the children of his town; he is also desirous that missionaries, and indeed settlers generally, should take up their abode with him.

Toto Korie, situated about ten miles east of Boporo, appears to me to be well adapted for a settlement; as a trading station it offers remarkable advantages, receiving as it does all the produce from the interior; the soil is suitable for all the requirements of a plantation, the situation seems healthy; stores, etc., can be brought up from the settlements in three days; and it is naturally of advantage to those who attempt to exercise a moral and educational influence over these people that their ruler should be well disposed toward projects of that kind, and apparently so well acquainted with the value of knowledge.   (Signed)

W WINWOOD READE.

The king has a frame house at Totoquella, with a piazza surrounding it, all of native construction. He also uses chairs, tables, beds, bedsteads, looking-glasses, scented soaps, colognes, etc. He took great interest in examining my sextant and even the pictures in my books; but that which afforded him the greatest pleasure was the stereoscope. He entreated me so earnestly to leave it with him, that I felt myself bound to gratify his wishes in that respect, though I had specially intended it for Musardu.

He was no less satisfied when I flattered him with the prospect of a school for children being established at Boporu telling me that when John B. Jordan traded there, he was accustomed to get Jordan to teach him.

The king spells a little, and is somewhat acquainted with numbers. This is the place for the missionary to be of service; but it seems that, though Mohammed has a small mosque and school at Vannswah, almost in the Virginia settlement, the Christians have neither church nor school at Boporu.

The king's authority seems to be of a mixed character. In some things he acts absolutely, while in others, such as war, he takes the counsel of the subordinate chiefs. He is judge or arbiter of all important differences between his subjects. He is a most patient hearer of all matters brought before him. I have known him to remain in his hammock for whole days, listening to what was to be said by either side, and his decisions seemed to be generally satisfactory.

A very peculiar but advantageous method obtains in the administration of justice. In order to obviate all further trouble after the decision is given, both plaintiff and defendant have to advance the cost and expenses before the suit begins: the very articles in which these charges are to be paid are placed in a conspicuous manner in the sight of everybody. The presence of the money thereby becomes an incentive and stimulation to strenuous effort. As soon as the case is decided, nothing remains but for the victor to sweep the stakes. These cases between his subjects are frequently taxing and vexatious, yet the king is said to always preside with patience and a well balanced impartiality.

But the king sometimes takes recreation from the severe affairs of life, at which time he is apt to enliven the hours of vacation from business with a glass of gin or whisky, and then he goes playfully around the town attended by his people. It happens that his caprice is as innocent then as his gentle disposition is in his sober hours, for he hurts no one; only going from house to house, joking with, and receiving little presents from his friends. Sometimes he attempts to dance, or to act some warlike feat; but want of youth and a rather fat body mar the practice. One day he insisted on the performance, to his no small discomfiture. He mounted himself upon an earthen hill, with a spear in each hand, in order to charge down in warlike style; starting in full tilt, he came sprawling to the ground with such violence as to scarify the royal bosom in a most unseemly manner.

Before I left Boporu for the interior, the king informed me that the distance, danger, and hazard were so great, that he must consult the sand-doctor as to the final issues of such a journey. He declared that upon all such important matters he trusted not to human pru dence alone.

This individual, the sand-doctor, by giving his fingers certain motions in a small pile of sand, is supposed to read the events of the future. We were carried into a thatch hut. Our diviner, spreading out a small pile of sand with his right hand began to invoke the demon of the pile. The whole thing was conducted without thunder, lightning, or any thing else, except the rapid, voluble utterances of our diviner himself. Again and again it was demanded of the flinty wisdoms whether or not the expeditions should be successful; the responses indicated by these sandy hieroglypics bid us begone and prosper. Thus it was that superstition at that time seconded the purposes of a rational inquiry. The king not unfrequently chided me because I was indifferent and incredulous about such matters.

Every effort was made by the Boporu Mandingoes to prevent my going, It was told to Momoru that if anything befell ue, he alone would be held responsible to the government. Even old Gatumba sent word to Momoru not to allow me, under any circumstances whatever, to pass and "go behind them;" for he declared that I was going for no other purpose but to ruin their trade. It was the first time, I was informed, that the king had set himself in opposition to the advice and counsel of his chiefs, many of whom were greatly opposed to my passing through their country to go in the interior I therefore exerted the greatest industry in purchasing their silence or assistance. But to the Boporu Mandingoes I held threatening language, in which I informed them that if I did not succeed in going to their country, I would return and break up all their trade at Vannswah.

Mr. Schieffelin's money, however, was the most powerful argument. It prevailed over every obstacle; it reconciled me to predjudices and persons the most difficult to deal with; invoked the blessings of Mohammed on my head; caused even the sands to become things of sense in my favor; singularly enlightened minds that could not see why I wished to go in the interior to the most undoubted moral certainty.

On the 14th of June, I left Boporu for Totoquella, and on June 16th, we left Totoquella for the interior, our company consisting of three Congoes—Jim, Alex, and Pickaninny—as carriers; Chancellor, the Golah, as interpreter, and Beah, the Mandingo, as guide. The rest of my Congoes, numbering fifteen, had returned to Monrovia, giving all kinds of false accounts of our proceedings.

I had now again to experience the effects of the jealousy of the Mandingoes. They had determined that I should not reach Musardu. They therefore gave secret instructions to the Mandingo guide, Beah, who was to accompany me, to delay and shuffle all along the route, so as to exhaust my means and discourage perseverance, and thus to finally thwart the expedition. It was through this man's tricks that I was compelled to spend six months in going to Musardu, when only one was necessary.

On Tuesday, the 16th of June, we left Totoquella for the interior, the direction being, with very little deviation, east. The hilly features of the country became more striking; large granite boulders were scattered here and there; small creeks, flowing over beds of sand and gravel, drained the country from every direction into the St. Paul's River About half-past four o'clock P. M., we reached the north-western edge of the Pessy country, and halted at a small hamlet for the night. Here the barometer stood 29.19; thermometer, 84°.

Wednesday, the 17th of June, six A. M., barometer, 29.20; thermometer, 78° Fahrenheit. We pushed on, and passed through another Pessy village. The Pessys seem to have an abundance of poultry, sheep, and rice; here we halted.

Thursday, the 18th of June, we started on our journey, the country bearing the same hilly appearance. We halted at a considerable village, called Sellayo, about twelve o'clock. The chief was swinging in his hammock in a half finished shed; he was sullen, and scarcely spoke; he, however, deigned to give us a little palm wine. We made him a small (dash) present, at which he was quite displeased; but we cut short all grumbling by starting off soon in the morning.

Friday, the 19th, we passed through Nesebeah (red hill) and Pollamah, Pessy villages, and halted at Zelliki's town at half past three P. M. This village contained 250 houses, built in the usual style; the body being of clay, with thatched conical coverings. This village wore an indifferent appearance, showing scarcely any activity in any species of industry On account of its sameness, we were glad enough to leave it. Outside of its barricade was a large creek containing catfish, as at Boporu.

The only thing that rendered the idle hours tolerable was King Momoru's daughter, who had married a Mandingo residing in the village. She very much resembled her father, and was of the same jovial disposition ; and when I left the village, she marched out before me, with my musket at shoulder-arms, at a military pace, imitating what she had seen at Monrovia the last time she was down there with her father.

Saturday, June 20th, 1868, we reached Barkomah, the largest Pessy town in this direction. King Pato is not stamped by nature for a king, and his town is neither commendable for cleanliness nor industry. It contains 300 dilapidated houses, half a dozen cows, some large Mandingo dogs, about 800 inhabitants, and is surrounded on all sides by impenetrable jungle, which is considered a sufficient barrier from all attacks. It is difficult to conceive whether this plan of defense was suggested by cowardice or laziness. We were lodged in a miserable little hut, about twelve feet long by eight feet wide, and five feet high. We had to endure this bamboo cage for ten days, because our guide had friends, who made him as comfortable as we were wretched. We were delayed under various pretexts, the chief of which was that, as my boys had almost given out, assistance had to be procured for carrying our luggage.

On the 1st of July, we started from Barkomah, and crossed a considerable tributary of the St. Paul's River, seventy-five feet wide, running in the direction of south-west between banks of clay, eight feet on one side and fifteen feet on the other, with a velocity of forty feet in fifteen seconds. The stream is ten feet deep in this place, and is known to overflow its banks on the eight-foot side in the depths of the rains. It is crossed on slender poles tied together. Only one person can cross at a time ; and just as the burdened traveler reaches the middle, he is arrested by a ticklish swaying that threatens to unbalance him into the waters below ; here he dares not move until the restive poles regain their quiet. It has blighted many a prospect, or rather melted many a basket of salt. In days gone by it was crossed by a suspension bridge of wicker work, elevated fifteen feet above the surface as appeared by the remains of logs and withes. This stream separates the Pessy country from the Deh country.

The Deh people are a small tribe intervening between the Pessy and Bonsie people. They seem to be a distinct people, and speak a strong rough, guttural language, similar to our Kroo tribe on the coast, whom they resemble in many other particulars. They have more fire in their eyes than the Pessy people, and are said to eat their enemies in war. After a half-hour's walk, we passed. through the Dey villages of Mue Zue and Yalah, and halted at Dallazeah. The Deh people. in proffering their hospitalities, offered us dog for dinner, which was politely declined.

On Thursday, the 2nd of July, we started from Dallazeah. Farms of rice, corn cotton, cotton, and tobacco succeeded each other in an order truly pleasing to look at. The people are very industrious. The women, on seeing me, began to tremble with fear ; and though some of my people, with whom they were well acquainted, tried to assure them, they could not be persuaded to approach me. Keeping the direction east, we passed another Deh village—Malung, (water). From here we came to the site of a large Deh town—Gellabonda, (lightning)—which had been completely destroyed by a civil war. It was so elevated that we had but to look E. S E to see a large part of the Barline country, and the very parts in which war was then raging. Indeed, we had hitherto followed the Barline route ; but at two o'clock P.M. our guide, Beah, changed the direction, remarking, as he did so, powder and ball were in the path he had left. We halted at Mahfatah, a small Deh village. At night, one of their houses caught on fire, and but for the activity of our people the whole of their frail Damboo dwellings would have been consumed. These people travel very little, and are consequently ruder, and as I then supposed, less hospitable than the other tribes. We passed the 4th of July here. the barometer standing at 28.89, thermometer 80° ; ten o'clock A. M., weather cloudy

Friday the 5th of July we started on our journey, passing through several Deh villages. We also crossed a small falls called Gawboah, with water rushing over granite beds colored red and gray, with seams of white quartz and red feldspar ramifying the bed in many directions. We halted at Zolaghee, the largest and last town of the Deh people. This town contained 300 houses, more or less in a state of dilapidation. Nothing is more disagreeable than to be obliged to take quarters in these decaying clay-built towns, especially in the rainy season, when the mud, trash, and all the soil, frogs, and vermin of the town dissolve, crumble, and creep too near not to annoy sensibilities accustomed to cleanliness. We managed to tolerate this town one day, in order to rest ourselves.

On the 7th, we reached the Bonsie country, or the Domar division of the Bonsies. We passed through Powlazue, Unzugahzeah, Kauli-

bodah, and halted at Yahwahzue.   These town are large and densely
peopled, surrounded with high and massive walls of clay and earth.
It was here that the Barline people had been lately making reprisals,
capturing the women and slaves on the farms It was therefore necessary that our Bonsie friends should exercise careful vigilance, and be
ready to sally forth from their walls at a moment's warning to repel
these incursions.

You no sooner arrive in a Bonsie country, than a contrast of cleanliness, order, and industry strikes you.   That tribe, continually represented to us as savage, fierce, and intractable, at once invites you into
its large walled towns with all the hospitalities and courtesy that the
minds of this simple, untutored people can think of.

I arrived at Zolu's town on the 8th of July, 1868, at four o'clock
P.M.   The walls of this town are from eighteen to twenty feet high,
consisting of clay, and very thick.   A regular salvo of musketry
announced my entrance, and quickly a band of music made its
appearance, consisting of twelve large and small ivory horns, and a
half dozen drums of various sizes and sounds.   I was conducted to
the market space, in the center of the town, and there welcomed
amidst the blast and flourish of Bonsie music and the firing of muskets.

They were astonished and overjoyed that (a Weegee) an American
should come so far to visit them in their own country.   A thousand
strange faces whom I had never before seen. were gazing at me. After
tneir curiosity and wonder had had been satisfied, they gave me spacious and comfortable lodgings and commenced a series of hospitalities which, from mere quantity alone, became oppressive.

The next day, my friends would have me put on American cloth ;
to please them, I did so.   I had not shaved for three months and
when I made my appearance in the 'Merican cloth, together with an
unshaven face, the women and children fled in every direction from
the frightfully bearded Weegee.   Many a Bonsie child was hushed to
silence or sleep by being threatened with the Weegee I annoyed the
women and children at such a rate, that I soon deemed it necessary
to take off the American cloth and the beard also.

This part of Africa likes a clean face, and especially a full flowing
gown, which is not only a more graceful attire, but more comfortable
and healthy than the tight-fitting pieces which we call civilized clothing.
This town, like Boporu, has its small daily market; but the large
weekly market, which is held every Thursday, and to which the neigh-

boring towns usually resort, is held at Zow Zow, a very large town fiteen miles E. N. E of Zolu. I visited this market. The hum of voices could be heard in the distance like the noise of a waterfall It is attended by five or six thousand people. The bargaining is generally conducted 'by the women, except the country cloth trade, which is carried on by the men. The exchange is generally a barter — one article is exchanged for another, to the mutual wants of the buyer and seller. Salt and kola, however, have the character of a currency, and large bargains are generally valued in these articles. They are the expression of prices in all important bargains. Kola usually performs the same service our coppers do in small bargains. These markets also have the character of holiday or pleasure-days Every one appears in his or her best attire. The women wear blue and colored country cloths girded tastefully around their waists their heads bound round with a large three-cornered handkerchief of the same material. Blue beads, intermixed with their favorite " pateriki " (brass buttons,) encircle their necks, their faces ornamented with blue pigment and smiles.

In going around the market, and even on the road as you go to the market, you are sure to be loaded with ground-nuts, bananas, and rice bread. Rice forms the chief breadstuff; cassavas and potatoes next. Potatoes grow to an enormous size, and will weigh from six to eight pounds. My Congo carriers were greatly elated when they bought a bushel of white rice for four brass buttons and a few needles. Considering the large farms and the quantities of old rice from the previous crop which must remain unconsumed, rice can never be a source of profit to these people until they have a road and conveyance to cart it down to some civilized settlement.

The two great farming staples in the Boozie country are rice and cotton. Sometimes the rice and cotton are planted together, but most of the cotton-farms succeed the rice farms. The cotton-farms bear no proportion in size to the rice-farms, yet they are large ; for they have to clothe a country densely populated, where men, women, and children all go clothed, and no foreign manufactures scarcely reach them. Cotton-gins would be a blessing to these people; for the manner in which they obliged to prepare cotton for spinning is painful and tedious to the last degree of labor. This part of the labor is done by the women ; the men do the weaving. The spindle is in the hands of every woman, from the princess to the slave. The dyeing of cloth is also done by the women; at which the Mandingoes are the most expert; and they know how to impart various shades of blue in a permanent and beautiful manner Though they have abundance of camwood I have never seen them use it for the purposes of dyeing. The chief colors used are blue and yellow; the latter color is extracted from bark Tak-into account that these people not only clothe themselves, but furnish the vast number of cloths that are brought to the coast to be used in the leeward trade, it shows what the cotton-producing power of the country would become if this primitive, barbarian industry were only assisted by some labor-saving machinery.

On the second day after my arrival, I had a musical compliment paid to me. A dozen young ladies, from ten to eighteen years of age, serenaded me in the following manner: A large mat being spread on the ground before my door, the young ladies seated themselves and commenced singing one of the songs of their country, marking the time, as well as accompanying the music, by means of hollow wooden pipes four and a half inches long, through which the wind is forced by beating one end with the palm of the hand. When this compliment is paid to a friend, one of the young ladies who has tact and talent improvises a solo as to his good qualities, his bravery, his good looks, his generosity, etc., at the conclusion of which all join the chorus, repeating the words, "Emmamow," "Emmamow,"— Thank you, thank you. It is also a very delicate way of insinuation, when your liberality does not always satisfy their expectations. My liberality in some cases "becoming small by degrees and beautifully less," a young lady revenged herself on me by singing that I had a "giving face but a stingy heart," at which they all responded, "Kella? Kella?"—Is it so? Is it so? Well, thank you; thank you. This is indeed a very delicate way of insinuation; but the ungenerous little rogue ought to have remembered that it was through my liberality that they were enabled to have all the fine brass buttons which they sported around their necks at the Zow Zow market. However, I hope it will be considered that I have done the state some service, when I announce that I have labeled nearly all the pretty women in the Boozie country as the property of the Republic of Liberia, with its military brass buttons, (pateriki).

The Boozies are a very polite people; the slightest favor is repaid with an "Emmamow"—Thank you. Do you dance or afford any amusement whatever, you receive the "Emmamow." Are you engaged in any labor or business for yourself or others. you are as heartily " thanked " by those whom it does not in the least concern as if it were for themselves. If you are carrying a heavy burden on the road, and happen to meet a friend, he thanks you as if you were doing it for him. My Congo carriers, who were nearly fagged out with their burd ns, used to be annoyed with this kind of civility, that contained all thanks and no assistance, and the Bonsie " Emmamow" was often exchanged for the Congo " Konapembo," (Go to the devil) an exhortation not unreasonable where misery is prolonged by politeness, and where one having his back bent, burdened, and almost broke, has to be stopped to be thanked and to snap fingers half a dozen times.

The soil of Zolu is chiefly a red sandstone, and the eastern road, worn down three feet by constant traveling and the successive wash-ings of the rains, exhibits to this depth their internal peculiarities— red sandstone, consolidated in proportion as the depth increases, but of crude and crumbling consistence at the surface, with ramifications of clear and distinct veins of white quartz from one to two and a half inches wide. On some of the hills there are large boulders of gran-ite, and some of them have markings crossing each other nearly in parallels in a direction from N. W. to S. E. and N. E. to S. W. The markings seem deeply ingrained, and are not so much sensible to the touch as visible to the eye. There is also in this country a stone of a very beautiful green color, capable of receiving a high pol-ish, a large piece of which was placed at the easteen gate of the town for a stepping-stone, and which, in that position from the frequent treadings it receives, had a finely polished surface. The character of the soil of the plains is principally clay and sand. The red sandstone at Zolu begins in the south-western portion of the Pessy country at the town called Nessebeah (red hill) ; and it is in this vicinity that the soil, changing from a mixture of clay and sand and granite pebbles, forms a red clayey and sandy composition. Nessebeah is located upon a very elevated hill of red clay and sand, which presents every grade of condensation, from a loose soil to solid rock. In the town were huge granite rocks, resting upon elevated beds of this red soil, as if they had been purposely placed there by human effort ; but they owe their position to some former power of nature and the subsequent washings of the rains. The elevation and position of these rocks serve to show what vast quantities of soil have been washed down in plains and valleys below Very extensive views are had from this site. The sides of the hills being rather steep the soil, on this account, is inclined to shelve down and to lay bare entirely its color and composition from the top to the bottom.   These red slopes form a curious contrast to the abundant green vegetation with which their summits and the plains below are clothed.

I arrived at Zolu on the 8th of July.   Here it was that the Mandingo guide, Beah. according to the instructions that had been given to him by King Momoru. was to spend a couple of weeks in trying to reconcile the differences between the Bonsies and the Barline people.   Zolu was also the town belonging to the young chief who had covertly assisted the Barline people, and who was now suffering the penalty of his perfidy.   He was confined at Salaghee, a large town fifteen miles east of Zolu, by a chief called Daffahborrah.

Three days after our arrival, Beah went to Salaghee, in order to open negotiations, both for the release of the young prince, Cavvea, and to stop the war between the Bonsies and Barlines.   King Momoru had already sent the same proposals for peace. His town being on the confines of the Boozie and Barline territory, was more subject on this account, to the incursions of the latter, and indeed on his town had fallen most of the brunt of the war.

Beah, after two days' absence at Salaghee, returned. He informed me that Daffahborrah had requested him not to bring me to his town, as he was afraid of the great war medicine which his people had told him I had in my possession. This war-medicine was a bottle of nitric acid, given me by Dr. Dunbar for the purpose of trying gold   My Congoes having witnessed some of its effects on cloth , metal, etc., had given it a fearful reputation: A tablespoonful scattered in a crowd would kill a hundred men; the least bit on a thatch house would burn up a whole town; I had but to stand outside the walls and throw it in the air to cause destruction to any town.   This bottle of "medicine" began to give me great inconvenience; everybody refused to carry it. A big bandage of rags and thatch housed the fiery spirit; great was the ceremony in assigning it its place wherever I happened to stop. Daffahborrah could not be blamed for refusing to see me.   Beah returned to Salaghee, and remained three weeks

It was now about the beginning of August, and the depth of the rains; I therefore determined to shun all exposure from the weather. What I particularly dreaded was the losing or damaging my instruments in crossing the creeks, with which a country rugged with every feature of hill and dale is everywhere intersected In the dries, many of them scarcely contain water enough to cover the foot; but in the rains they become torrents, eight and ten feet deep, with a swift and destructive current, being in fact, drains or gullies tilted toward the main reservoirs the St. Paul's and Little Cape Mount rivers. The rains had fairly set in; yet the quantity of water is much less than what I have been accustomed to experience on the seaboard at Monrovia.

The country is every variety of hill, plain and valley Standing upon an elevation it seemed to me that the people had attempted to cover the whole country with their ricefields. Toward the west could be seen the rice hills enveloped in showers ; succeeding that, whole mountain-sides of rice partly buried in vapor ; next to that could be seen a brilliant sunlight, spread over the brown and ripening plains of rice below.

It would be difficult to decribe into how many scenes sunshine, showers, clouds, and vapor can vary a locality, itself an expression of every variety of change.   Only here and there could be seen patches of large forest trees.   So completely had this section of the country been farmed over and over, that only saplings of three or four years' growth covered the uncultivated parts.   Nor will they be allowed to attain a greater age or size before the requirements of agriculture will clear them for rice and cotton-fields.

This is the chief reason why all the barricades or walls of towns, in this section of the country, are formed of earth and clay, instead of the large stakes that are used by the natives living in the vicinity of Liheria.

The Bonsie people have very tractable dispositions, and are wedded to no particular species of error.   Fetichism has no strong hold on them.   They believe in that thing most that manifests the greatest visible superiority of power. They are greatly duped by the fraud and chicanery of the Mohammedan Mandingo priests.

In general physical appearance the Boozies are well built generally from five and a half to six feet high in stature, with stoutly developed bodies, of sufficient muscular strength to hold a United States musket, bayonet fixed, at full arm's length in one hand They are an exceedingly healthy people, and of very clean habits. They bathe regularly twice a day, night and morning, in warm water, besides the intermediate cold water baths they are sure to take at whatever creek they happen to cross in their daily walking. For cleaning the teeth, they use a brush made of ratan, admirably adapted to the purpose.

Paring the finger and toe-nails is carried to excess. And the women at Zolu are foolish enough to pluck away part of their eyebrows and eyelashes, things which nature had not too lavishly furnished them from the first.

Many of the women are very pretty ; and for the many faces with which I am acquainted at Monrovia resemblances, and close resemblances, are to be found among the Boozie. Most of our people at Monrovia are fond of deriving themselves from the Mandingoes. I am sorry to say that this Boozie type of resemblance does not confirm an origin so noble and consoling. We must therefore rest satisfied with humbler antecedents.

As soon as the weather permitted traveling, I insisted on Beah resuming the journey. But he framed many excuses. and finally, to rid himself of my importunities ran off to Bokkasah, where his family resided. Thither I dispatched one of my boys, demanding his return ; but he refused to come. Beah was trying to carry out the secret instructions he had received from the Boporu Mandingoes. To trammel and obstruct my going still more. he sent word to the Boozies at Zolu that they were not to allow me to go anywhere ; for if any thing befell Momoru's American man, they alone would be held responsible for it. Three times I endeavored to leave this town ; but the people, by entreaties, presents, and every means of persuasion they could think of, compelled me to relinquish my intentions.

Beah had duped them as to the real reasons of delay Finally, it was appointed that if Beah should not return in two weeks, I was to go anvwhere I chose. The time expired without Beah's making his appearance.

On Monday, September 21st, 1868, I left Zolu, and went to Fissahbue, a town in latitude 7° 56′ 09″ N., and longitude 9° 50′ 43″ W. I was now entirely abandoned by my Mandingo guide, to grope my way to Musardu by inquiry or instinct.

Fissahbue is a double town. or a town partitioned into two parts, occupied in one by the Mandingoes, and in the other by the Boozies. It is well built and clean in appearance, with a population of three thousand inhabitants. The king, Mullebar, is a fine looking old gentleman of fifty years, very generous-hearted, and who was the more interesting to me because he had an equal dislike to Beah.

On Saturday, September 26th, we left Fissahbue for Bokkasah. The rough features of the country moderated into extensive plains of long fields of grass, ferns and tall palms; the hills were at a short distance, trending along in a direction west and north-west. They had also changed the character of their formation from red sandstone to granite, and I was struck to see these round and bossy masses, with their water-courses, shining and trickling down their slopes. Some of their tops were thickly wooded, while small tufts or patches of grass were thinly scattered on their sides; but its brownish appearance showed that the sun had parched it in its stony bed at the first approach of the dries. West of Bokkasah, granite hills rose one above another, crowned with a dense forest. Whenever it rained, a noise resembling distant thunder was always heard In the months of July and August, these hills are the site of a roaring cascade.

On the road, we fell in with people from all the neighboring towns, going to market. Sitting on the roadside were numbers of young women with baskets of ground-nuts already shelled, offering them for sale. Our pockets and every other available place were immediately filled, gratis. Such is their custom to strangers ; and their gift was particularly enhanced by the repeated liberality with which both hands went down into the basket, and came up piling full, to be emptied with a gracious smile into the capacious pockets of our country coats. Then followed an exchange of compliments ; and the three languages— Boozie, Mandingo, and English—got into a confusion from which smiles and brass buttons alone could deliver us.

On we went, munching ground-nuts and receiving ground-nuts, snapping fingers and making friends, and occasionally consigning Beah to evil destinies. At last the road suddenly widened, broad and clean ; and the din of human voices assured us that we had come upon the market and the town.

Bokkasah is in latitude 8° 10′ 02″. It is a double town, similar to Fissahbue, one part of which is Boozie, and the other Mandingo. The walls that contain the Boozie portion of the inhabitants make a circuit completely oval. That which comprises the Mandingoes butts up against and flanks the eastern side of the Boozie walls, and is also half oval in shape.

On entering the town, we were shown Beah's residence. Astonished at our arrival, he forthwith tried to make some slight atonement for his former shortcomings by the diligence with which he procured us comfortable lodgings. We were soon domesticated in the town,

kindling up friendships on all sides.   The Mandingoes made it a
point to be foremost in all these alliances.   Since I was going to their
country, they took me in their special charge.   Among the many at-
tentions paid me, I was invited by a young Mandingo lady to go with
her to see her mother.   We had no sooner arrived at the house, than
she commenced calling out, "Ma, ma !"   I waited to hear what
would follow ; but the next words were in musical Mandingo, inform-
ing her mother that she had brought the Tibbabue (American man)
to see her.   The Mandingoes use the same words in calling mother
that we do.   This interview ended satisfactorily in a large bowl of
rice, with fried chicken, palm-wine, etc., together with a standing invitation to come to her house every day while I remain in Bokkasah.

The young lady was married to a young Mandingo by the name of
Fatomah, whose father, Phillakahmah, resided at Boporu, but was
then in the Barline country.   The kindness and good office of this
family were untiring.   I also had many friends in the eastern part of
the town, who were constant in their attention to me.

Bokkasah contains about fifteen hundred houses, and about seven
thousand inhabitants.   It is very perplexing on the first entrance of
a stranger to find his way in these towns ; for the houses seem to be
dropped by accident into their places, rather than placed after any
organized method.   Chancellor, my interpreter, though well accustomed to these kind of towns, was not at all times assured of his own
whereabouts.   A woman gave him water to bathe ; after he had performed his ablutions, he found himself naked, lost, and ashamed to
ask where he was.   He wandered over the town with the vessel in his
hand, until some one guessing the truth, brought him home.   One
does not lose his way on account of the size of these towns, but
on account of the manner in which the houses are sprinkled about.
You can march up to your house without knowing it, so completely
does similarity and confusion repeat itself.

The market of Bokkasah which is held every Saturday, is one of
the principal markets in the Domar country.   It is also a great country cloth market.   In all these markets throughout the Boozie and
Barline countries, the small country cloth known among us as the trade
country cloth is not to be seen.   It is is owing to the mischievous industry of our friends at Boporu and its vicinity that these country
cloths are reduced to so small a size.   It is the business of these in-
terlopers in trade to take large country cloths to pieces, and make
them smaller.   Similar is their dealing with every species of trade, to

its great diminution and discouragement. If the interior trade amounted to millions of dollars in value to the republic, it could never reach our seaport towns while the border of our influence has been removed by tribal interference and war, and confined to the very seacoast settlements themselves. These obstructions can only be removed by the energetic action of government.

Bokkasah is a town very convenient and cheap for living. Abundance of vegetables, rice, beans, potatoes, plantains, bananas, ground-nuts, etc., are to be had at all times at the daily market.

While I was staying here, I dispatched one of my Congoes to Begby. a Mandingo chief, living at a town called Bokkadu, near the Boondee country, in a westward direction. As he was anxious to see some one who had come from an American town, and in American dress I tried to grati y him in that respect This Congo, before he rea hed Bokkadu crossed the St. Paul's River on a bridge of wicker-work, and the Cape Mount River which was much wider, on a corkwood float. This journey occupied three days. Both of these rivers flow from the northeast.

Among some of the singular institutions that prevail in this country is a kind of convent for women, in the mysteries of which every woman has to be instructed. What these mysteries are I have never been fully informed. They consist in the main of a peculiar kind of circumcision and of certain other practices necessary to health. Attached to the outer wall of the town are the houses, fenced in on all sides from the gaze of passers-by, and especially excluded against the entrance of men. It is death to any man to be caught within the precincts, which is instantly inflicted without reprieve by the women themselves.

There are, however, holidays in which the rigid rules of the institution are relaxed, and every body is permitted to go in and see their friend without distinction of sex. During my stay here, one of these holidays occurred, and I was invited to visit the sacred grounds of this female mysticism. It consisted of rows of long huts built low to the ground, the lodgings of the devotees. Each complement belonging to a hut were seated in a line, in front of their dwellings, on a mat. Their heads were wound round with enormous turbans, and their bodies decked out in all the finery their friends in town could afford. They kept their heads hanging down in a solemn manner. Even children, six or seven years of age, were included in this moping, surly observance. Their friends from town crowded around, delighted at the sight, and with unfeigned pleasure asked me if it was not fine. I should have been more pleased to have heard these women and children laughing and singing in their rice and cotton-farms, than to have seen them tormenting themselves with a senseless, morose custom. I was carried into one of their establishments and made to shake hands with my moody sisters

As I have before related this was the town in which my Mandingo guide, Beah, and all his family resided. Three days after my arrival, he disappeared, pretending he had immediate business at Salaghee, leaving word with the town-people not to allow me to go anywhere until he returned. I was determined to free myself from his tricks, and I exposed to his friends his dealings with me when I was at Zolu. His friends, and especially his mother and sisters besought me to wait for him. After a week had expired, I grew impatient to start; but the whole family of women came, crossing their hands, and placing themselves in the most suppliant attitudes, crying, "Ejung Ejung" —I beg you! I beg you! These poor women were honest, and knew nothing of their relation's crooked dealings. They made use of various ways to reconcile me to further delay. I had now been at Bokkasah three weeks, and had been foiled in every attempt to get away. The sort of hinderances through which I had now to struggle were not downright tyrannical opposition; they were of a more powerful and moral kind; supplications based upon kindness and generosity.

About this time an old Mandingo priest whom I had met at Bessa's town arrived. After he had been in town two days, he sent for me, and appeared glad to see me. I related to him the difficulties I experienced from Beah's actions. He advised me to be careful, and not to force my way through the country, as there had been a plot made to hurt me; and he went on to make many dark and pregnant insinuations. He exhorted me to patience and prayer, the contraries of which I had been provoked to by the artifices of Beah, and the consequent delays he had occasioned me. The next day the Mandingo priest told me that I had better make a "Sallikah," which is an offering to good luck. This offering was dictated by the priest himself. It was to be a sheep a penknife, a white country cloth, and ten white kola. Not knowing what divinity was to be appeased, I refused to make the sacrifice or oblation; for this priest was subsisting on a dry vegetable diet, the hospitality of his stingy brethren, and he was poor, very poor. The sacrifice or offering was to be delivered to him to be buried in the ground. But who could not see the crafty old priest and his hungry students in a congratulatory chuckle over a fat sheep, a penknife, a country cloth, and a fool of a Tibbabue?

This sort of priest is numerous, needy, cunning, and mischievous ; they distribute themselves in all the towns between Musardu and Boporu ; and they did not fail to present themselves to me throughout the journey as "god-men." But I gave them plainly to understand that I was not to be gulled by their practices.

I now dissembled my anxiety to depart, putting on a semblance of cheerfulness to abide where I was, and a perfect indifference about going anywhere. Every afternoon I would dress myself in my Mandingo toga, and go in the eastern part of the town to visit my friends. Here we would fritter away the time in talking and singing, and I musically entertained several of my Mandingo friends with the beauties of "Dixie." We would then clap into our prayers, they repeating the Fatiha, and I reciting the Lord's Prayer. A young lady begged that I would write off this prayer for her, in order that she might have it to wear around her neck, as well as to have fillets made of it to bind around her temples, as she was sometimes troubled with the headache. I wrote it off for her ; but I made her understand, at the same time, that its efficacy consisted in healing the ailments of the soul and not of the body. While we were thus handsomely enjoying ourselves, the terrible Dowilnyah sent his messengers for me to come and see him.

Dowilnyah is the king of the Wymar Boozies. His messengers were tall black men, with red and restless eyes, tattooed faces, filed teeth, huge spears, and six feet bows. They also had a reputation which remarkably corresponded with their appearance.

A discussion arose as to the safety of my going, and it caused a disagreement that ended in the return of the messengers without me. In a week's time the messenger's returned again. I had resolved to go with them. But my friends did all they could to dissuade me. Many of Dowilnyah's atrocities were repeated to me ; how, when he had suspected the fidelity of one of his wives he compelled her to pound the child of her supposed illicit connection in a mortar ; how he had wantonly shot one of his wives, remarking, as he did so, that he had only shot a dog ; his terrible cruelty to his prisoners whom he captured in war ; and even his cruelty to his own children, one of whom he threw among the drivers, (*termites bellicosi,*) and which was so mutilated by these voracious insects that the child lost one of its arms. He had no peer in cruelty and wickedness except Comma, who was now dead, but who, when living, went hand in hand with him in evil deeds. Comma's town, it must be remembered, was the place where Seymore had his right hand nearly slashed off

I, however, left Bokkasah for Dowilnyah's on Monday, the 2d of November, 1868, and arrived at Ukbaw Wavolo, a village at which he was residing, on Thursday the 5th of November, 1868.

Before reaching this village, we halted in our journey, at Nubbewah's town. It was well built, clean, and strongly fortified. We were brought into the presence of Nubbewah, the chief. He was an old man; tall, or rather long—as he was lying down—thin, and looked to be much emaciated by sickness. It was difficult to arouse him from the lethargic insensibility into which he had fallen. His attendants, however, succeeded in awakening him to the fact of our presence ; but, as we still seemed to be regarded as a dream, I thought proper to quicken his consciousness by blazing away with my revolver against his earthen walls. This act perfectly startled him into a proper regard for our dignity and welfare, and thereupon we are well fed, comfortably lodged, and liberally presented with mats and country cloths, etc.

On Wednesday, we traveled until we reached Boe, a very large town belonging to the Wymar Boozies. This town, with some outlying villages, is the beginning of the Wymar country which is separated from the Domar by a narrow creek, acknowledged as a boundary. The village where the king was staying is E N. E., of Boe, and about two and a half hours' walk from that town.

A temporary misunderstanding between the king and some of his his chiefs had caused him to reside in this secluded hamlet.

It appears that Boe had been threatened with an attack from the Domar Boozies. Succor was immediately requested from Dowilnyah, who quickly marched from his capital, Gubbewallah, to the defense of Boe He succeeded in defeating the Domars. But during his residence at Boe, so overshadowing was his influence and power, that the subordinate chiefs found themselves nearly stripped of the authority they were accustomed to exercise. A general dissatisfaction ensued, on which the king became so indignant that he withdrew from Boe, drawing in his train every thing that rendered the town attractive and important. He remained deaf to every solicitation to return. And here, at this village, he held his court, giving audience to the messengers of interior chiefs, granting favors, adjusting disputes. The village was alive with the chiefs of other towns, messengers going and coming, fine-looking women, warriors, etc.

When we drew near the village, we were requested by our guides to discharge our pieces in order to inform the king of our arrival. This being done, we entered. The king, seated on a mat, was dressed in a gaudy-figured country robe; on his head was a large blue and red cloth cap, stuck all over with the talons of large birds. At his side was seated his chief counselor, whose name was Jebbue, a man of very large proportions, but of a mild and gentle countenance. The king was surrounded by his people, all variously dressed in white, blue striped and yellow country coats.

His countenance assured us that he had not been misrepresented, notwithstanding his effort to compose it in a peaceful manner. It was one of the most threatening and the blackest visages I had seen for some time. He bade me welcome. A mat was then spread, upon which we seated ourselves. Suddenly his iron horns and drums sounded, his warriors rushed forth from their concealed places, performing all the evolutions of a savage and barbarous warfare. The thundering plaudits of the people themselves increased the din. After this tremendous flourish had subsided, the king arose, and, stepping forward, he waved his right hand in all directions, announcing by that gesture the uncontrolled authority with which he reigned in his dominions. Being welcomed again and again to his country, we were shown to our lodgings, which, though just temporarily erected, were comfortable.

Friday, 6th of November, 1898, I visited the king. Stating that we had come to see his country and to make ourselves acquainted with him and his people, we then delivered our presents, which consisted of a piece of calico ; a music-box, with which he was especially pleased ; two pocket handkerchiefs, 1 pair epaulets, two bottles cologne, one clasped knife, three papers needles, one large brass kettle. He was delighted ; he told me that I should not regret my visit to his country ; and come who would after me, I should always hold the first place in his estimation ; that he had been informed of all that had been said against him to prevent my coming to see him ; but as I had disregarded these reports, he would show me that my confidence had not been misplaced.

He was anxious to see my revolvers, the fearful reputation of which preceded me everywhere I went. They were shown ; their use explained and their effect exaggerated. When he had also seen the astronomical instruments, his courage entirely forsook him. He requested me to give him some medicine to prevent his enemies from poisoning him.

I replied that I had no such medicine ; that by exercising the proper precaution in eating and drinking. he might be able to escape the evil intention of his enemies.

He next requested me to fire my muskets, that he might see the mysteries of a cap-gun ; and he caused all the broken pieces of the exploded caps to be gathered and preserved. I had to take some pains to dismiss his apprehensions that I would hurt him in any way.

He celebrated my visit to his country by a war-dance. It commenced it with some of his old habits, in which, however, palm wine flowed instead of blood. After he had supped off about a quart of that beverage, he retired to his residence, and in the lapse of fifteen minutes, the clamor of his people and his war-drums signified his reappearance. He came forward with wild and prodigious leaps ; a war-cap of leopard skin, plumed with horse hair, covered his head ; he was naked to the waist, but wore a pair of Turkish-shaped trowsers. He had a large spear in his right hand. His dress and enthusiasm had completely metamorphosed him. His black and lowering countenance had undergone a terrible change, which was heightened by the savage grin which his white teeth imparted to it. The most frantic gestures now took place, amid the stunning plaudits of the whole town.

This being ended, the king called upon his women to give the finishing stroke to this happy business.

The ladies of Wymar are fond of dancing, and they spend much of their time in this amusement : they are not acquainted with the polite and delicate paces of their sisters at Monrovia ; but for downright solid-footed dancing, they can not be surpassed. They are all fine, large, robust women, and have the happiest looking countenances in the world.

African rulers in these parts travel very leisurely from one point to another, and at every intermediate place where they may halt, are sure to spend as much time as would be necessary to carry them to their final destination. This careless, lounging habit of wasting time is an incurable one ; arguments or persuasion strengthened by gifts can not overcome it.

The king had informed me of his intention to leave the village for his own town ; the very day was appointed. He did not leave, however, until two days afterward. On Tuesday, 10th November, the king requested me to fire my muskets, in order to announce to the neighboring towns and villages his departure.

He preferred my guns, because their report was louder than the cracking of his little English fusees, many of which I was assured had come to him by the way of Musardu through the Mandingoes.

At ten o'clock we started, the king being attended by his friends, body-guard, musicians, and women   Happily the town to which we we were going lay on the road direct to Musardu. About three o'clock we came to Ziggah Porrah Zue, the largest town and the capital of the Wymar country.   The king before entering the town made a halt to put on his robes. Everybody dressed themselves. I was even requested to put on my uniform, which I did. After much firing and music, we entered, amid the applause and gaze of the whole town.   After we had passed the gate and traversed the town some distance, we found ourselves encountered by another gate and wall; this contained the middle town. We passed on, and soon arrived at the gate and wall of the central town.   Thus there are three towns, with their walls concentrically arranged. The inner walls were, however, much dilapidated, and served only to show in what manner the whole town had been successively enlarged ; for as soon as an outside wall had been built around the new outside town, the inner wall was suffered to decay. The exterior or outside wall, though of great extent, was in good repair.   We were conducted to the market-space in the central town, which was spacious and convenient for holding large crowds.   Some arrangement and order being introduced, a speech of welcome was delivered by the old chief of the town, Dowilnyah's uncle. At the conclusion, every trumpet, consisting of forty pieces, sounded. The band of ivory and wood belonged to the town ; and it must be confessed that though the execution was simple, in effect it was really fine. Many speeches were made, the end of which was always concluded with music from the bands.   These three bands did not all play at the same time, but successively, one after another, the king's band being allowed the precedence.

After speech-making came the war-dances of the principal chiefs, the women cheering them on.   Each chief, as soon as he had performed his part, was immediately saluted by the king's body-guard, who, marching forward to meet him, acknowledged by that act his valor and achievements.   Dowilnyah closed the festivities by exhibiting his own warlike prowess. We were assigned our lodgings. Every day we passed in this town was given to festivity and enjoyment.

One of their chief amusements was a "jack upon stilts," a fellow fantastically dressed, wearing a false face, and mounted upon stilts ten feet high fitted to the soles of his feet—with which he danced, leaped, and even climbed upon the houses. He was full of clownish tricks and sayings, and made much sport for the crowds; he belonged to the king's train, a sort of king's fool. The women are really the industrious part of the population; for while their lords are wholly devoted to pleasure, palavers, and wars, the women are engaged in numerous domestic duties, and especially in spinning cotton. Here, also, as in the Domar country, the spindle is in the hands of every woman, from the princess to the slave. The women however, enjoy themselves, particularly on market days, which at this town takes place every Sunday.

This market is seated on the banks of the St. Paul's River. and is carried on under the shade of a large cotton (bombax) and acacia-trees. The commodities of exchange are country cloths, cotton stripes, raw cotton, iron soap, palm-oil, palm-butter. ground-nuts, rice, plaintains, bananas, dried fish, dried meat, peas, beans, sweet potatoes, onions (chalots) snuff tobacco, pipes, salt, earthern pots or vessels for holding water and for cooking purposes, large quantities of Kola slaves, and bullocks. The bullocks are generally brought by the Mandingoes to the market. Palm-wine is not allowed to be sold in the market. Peace and order are secured by persons especially appointed for that purpose. After every body has assembled on the ground, these preservers of the peace with long staves in their hands go through the market, ordering every body to sit down; they then admonish the people to carry on their bargains peacefully and without contention. This preliminary being gone through with the market is opened. It is generally attended by six or seven thousand people. There are several large markets held in the Wymar country; the one at Comma's town is larger than this. The daily market held in the central town is very convenient for making small purchases.

On Saturdays, sitting under the shade of large acacia-trees, I have watched the almost uninterrupted stream of people with their bundles and packs coming from every neighboring town and village to market. The bridge crossing the St Paul's River would be laden or occupied from one end to the other, for hours, but it proved equal to the purpose for which it was built. When the Mandingoes would arrive with their cattle they would swim them across, but always experience difficulty in getting them up this side of the bank, on account of its steepness. No one seemed to think of remedying this inconvenience by sloping a pathway for the animals.

The bridge is a simple structure of wicker-work. From each side of the river the ends of the bridge depend from a stout branch of an acacia-tree The roadway is of plaited ratan, two feet wide, and worked up on both sides about four and a half feet. to prevent falling over. It is further steadied and supported by a great number of strong and flexible twigs which connect the bottom and the sides to every available limb of the trees growing on each bank. It is ascended by ladders ; its elevation is from twenty three to twenty-five feet from the surface of the river, and spans a length of eighty-five feet.

Ziggah Porrah Zue, the capital of the Wymar country is in latitude 8° 14′ 45″ ; longitude 9° 31′. Its elevation is about 1650 feet above the level of the sea.   The barometer standing from 28 o8 to 28.12. Thermometer ranging from 67° to 92° from November 14th to November 30th. It is seated on the St. Paul's River. The large market is held between the river and the wall of the town. I am informed that this river runs N E. by E. into the Mandingo country, and that it takes its rise at the foot of some hills in that country. The Little Cape Mount River takes a similar direction ; but in point of size, and in the number of its tributary creeks, it is superior to the St. Paul's.

The highest point of the slope or declivity of land from Monrovia to Ziggah Porrah Zue is from 1600 to 1700 feet above the level of the sea for a distance of latitude 115 miles. It is impossible that rivers thus situated should be any thing else but the drains of a country, and their course a series of cataracts and falls.

Every afternoon the king's body-guard performed their military evo lutions. They had three war-drums, one of which was bound around with three tiers of human jaw-bones. A double quick was beaten, to which they kept time for about half an hour, without tiring. They would then enter upon more violent motions, which were more of an athletic than a military kind. They were armed with English fusees, and heavy iron cutlasses of native manufacture. Their war-dress consisted of leopard-skins.

The Bonsie country is densely populated. The difference between the Domar and Wymar Boozie is, that the latter marks his face from the temple to his chin with an indellible blue stain, while the former does not practice tattooing of any kind. The tribe extends from the south-west portion of the Pessy country to the western border of the Mandingo country.

Dowilnyah now proposed to forward me on to Musardu under his protection—and a more powerful protection could not be obtained. His own nephew was to accompany me. We left Ziggah Porrah Zue November 30th, 1868, taking a direction E. N. E: The country was open and covered with tall grass, cane-brake, and wild rice. In an hour's walk we came to the town where the king formerly resided, Gubbe-wallah, meaning Sassa-wood tree, referring to a large old tree that grew in the middle of the town.

We passed on, and halted at Pellezarrah—meaning several paths, because several paths crossed each other near the town.

Several large cotton-trees grew at the junction of the roads. The features of the country are hilly but the slopes are longer and more gentle. One large hill had a gradual slope of nearly two miles, while its opposite side came down in a perpendicular line. Tress now indeed began to be scarce, the country being covered with cane-brake, wild rice, and very tall palm trees. Some trees of that short, stunted species which grow on our beach at the Cape, were seen sparsely scattered here and there. We traveled over a hard soil of red clay, pebbles, and iron ore. The tall grass and treeless slopes, plains, and hills led my Congoes to declare that I had missed the route, and walked into the Congo country ; and they commenced to thank me for returning them into their country Mesumbe. We halted at Pezarrah at six o'clock P. M. This town had suffered from fire in one part and was rebuilt The whole direction traveled was E N. E. Tuesday, 1st December, 1868, we started from Pellazarrah. After a walk of a quarter of an hour, the road led through a district which was a solid mass of iron ore. A short reddish grass struggled for existence on this extensive plain of metal. The iorn was so pure that the road leading through it was a polished metal pathway, smothed over by the constant treading of travelers. It is said to be hardly treadable in the dries, it becomes to thoroughly heated.

We occupied three and a half hours in passing over these hills and plains of me al. We afterward came to high grass, through which some elephants had just passed. The palm-trees entirely cease. We halted at Ballatah at three o'clock P. M.

Wednesday, 2d December, 1868, at Ballatah. This is one of the most pleasantly situated of all the Boozie towns we had visited The people insisted on our spending a day with them, that they might have some time to look at us. They killed a sheep, and furnished rice and other things in abundance. They then tried to prevail on me to undertake an elephant-hunt with them. Elephants are plenful and large in this portion of the country and every night they could be heard making a noise, while regarding themselves on the tender cotton-plants growing in the farms of the Ballatah people.

Artemus Ward declares that "Every man has his own fort." It is not mine to hunt eleghants—especially in going to hunt elephants going in herds of ten or twelve, and that in an open country like Ballatah. I therefore declined the invitation to go on an elephant-hunt, telling my friends that I would postpone the pleasure to be derived from such amusements until I returned from Musardu.

Ballatah is in latitude 8° 17′ 51″. Its approximate elevation is about two thousand feet above the level of the sea; barometer standing 27.172. It is not so large as the other Boozie towns but far better laid out. The houses are not crammed so closely together. It contains about twenty-five hundred people; it is seated in a plain, and is commanded by very high and abrupt hills on its western side, while the land rolls off in gentle undulations toward the east. We were carried to some outlying villages northwest of Ballatah, situated at the foot of the same high hills that overlook that town. Here they were busy smelting iron The furnaces were built of clay, and of a conical shape, from five and a half to six feet high having clay pipes or vents close to the bottom arranged in groups of two and three, for the purpose of draught. The charcoal and iron ore are put in at the top. At the bottom is an opening through which the slag and other impurities are withdrawn

Thursday, December 3rd, 1868, we started from Ballatah. The direction was N.E., and parallel to a range of very high hills, called the Vukkah hills. These hills are from seven hundred to one thousand feet high and are variously composed of granite, iron ore, and a reddish clay which, from the steep slopes near the top, had shelved down in many places. The whole country, hill and plain, was covered with long grass and canebrake, interspersed with a short, dwarfish tree. The bark of this tree is rough and corrugated, the trunk is a foot in circumference, eight or ten feet high; it has an excessive branching top. The leaves small, and of an oval shape. Clumps of large trees occupied the sides and knolls of the hills.

These hills are of all sizes, and run in every direction. Toward the N. and N.E , a line of hills towers above the rest, the ridge of which makes a variety of outline against the sky These hills are not so ruggedly disposed as those in the Domar country. The slopes are entler; only near the summit they sometimes change feature, taper off to a point, or go right up perpendicularly. To these hills and fastnesses the natives resort in time of war, carrying all their effects, their wives and children, to the most inaccessible parts. Judging from a hill which was shown me as being used for that purpose, some of them must be very safe retreats.

Agriculture in this country must be a very simple and easy process. No "cutting farm," as we call it, by felling trees and cutting undergrowth. The soil, though covered with tall grass and canebrake, is one of the highest fertility. When the sun has sufficiently parched the tall grass, it is sometimes burnt off, sometimes cut down and hoed in for manure. Farms of hundreds of acres can be prepared in a very short time; and the natives, with their small hoes, can well afford to have the large plantations of rice, cotton, and millet, which we saw.

Friday, 4th of December, 1868, we rested at Vukkah. This town stands at the foot of a range of high hills of the same name. It is the last Boozie town, and the nearest to the Mandingo country. These hills, called "Vukkah" by the Boozies, and "Fomah" by the Mandingoes, take a definite direction N. E. They are the highest range, and form a marked and acknowledged boundary between the Boozie and Mandingo territories. At the foot of this range are seated a number of towns, Boozie and Mandingo.

The town of Vukkah was overgrown with wild cane and plaintain-trees. The houses were dilapidated, presenting a disagreeable contrast to the usual neatness of the Boozie towns. The inhabitants are the most ill-favored of all the Boozies This town is also notorious for the mischief and trouble it gives thoroughfarers; and but for our coming under the protection of Dowilnyah, it soon fell out what would have happened. We had not been in the town an hour before we had a row with one of the principal men of the place. He requested me to fire my musket, which I did a number of times, sufficient, as I thought, to please every body; but he insisted on several more rounds. I refused; he then told me to go on to Musardu, but when I returned I would find that my way home would not lie through that town. I was, however, under too powerful a protection to be disturbed Dowilnyah was not to be trifled with. To take a head from a shoulder was mere pastime with him.

Much allowance, however, must be made for these African rulers. Tyrannical and bloodthirsty they sometimes appear; but this character is artificial, and practiced in many instances to inspire terror and respect, without which they could not hold their authority a single hour.

Beset by rivalships and conspiracies, they are forced, from the bois-
terous circumstances of their situation, to employ every means conservative of their authority and their lives.

Saturday, 5th of December, we started from Vukkah. We had now
crossed the Vukkah hills, and were fairly in the Mandingo country.
Many of the plains of this section of the country are terraced, one
above another. Amends is made for a simple vegetation, by the ever-
varying forms of relief the country presents, the farther you advance
into it.

At 3 o'clock P. M., we were met on the road by several Mandingoes, who accompanied us to their town, Nu-Somadu or Mahommadu. The walls of this town are quadrilateral in shape, each side
being a series of bastions, which at a distance looks like some old
fortified front. The walls, however, are so thin that a four-pounder
could demolish them in a very little time.

We entered the town, and were entertained in a very hospitable
manner. A house was given to us, small indeed in its dimensions to
what we had been accustomed to in the Boozie country, but convenient and comfortable. Being wearied with the journey, I threw myself into a hammock and commenced surveying alterations and arrangements which a change in the character of the country had introduced. The house was a circular structure of clay, with a conical
roof made entirely of large canebrake and long grass. In looking
around the wall, our eyes rested on a saddle, stirrups, bridle, with
leather leggings, and a tremendous tower gun.

Sunday, the 6th of December, we attempted to pursue our journey;
but the chief refused to allow us to depart before he had demon-
strated his good will and hospitality. He killed a heifer and cooked
it with onions. We satisfied our appetites and made him an appro-
priate present. We then departed; arrived at Naalah late in the
afternoon. In the morning, a trooper was at once dispatched to
Musardu to inform them that the Tibbabue (American) had come.
In two hours he returned, telling me that the Musardu people requested that I would remain at Naalah until they had made preparations
for my reception. I immediately sent them word that I had been so
long coming to see their country that I would rather forego any public demonstration than be delayed any further. I was then answered
to come on, they would gladly receive me.

Accompanied by several Mandingoes from Naalah and Mahommadu, we started for Musardu. Our interest in the journey was en-

livened by the novel features of the country.   In passing through the
Boozie country extensive views were frequently obstructed by a dense
vegetation that hemmed in the sight on each side of a narrow foot-
path.   Here the peculiar features of the country are visible for miles.
The towns and villages seated in the plains, people on foot and people
on horseback can be seen at a great distance, and have more the air
of light, life and activity, than many parts of the Boozie country,
where the sombre gloom of immense forests conceals all such things
The large town of DuQuirlelah lay on our right, in the bosom of
some small hills.   It lay on our right; but from our elevated position,
it might well be said to lie under us.   Going on, we descried a long
whitish border, raised a little above the height of a gentle slope.   On
drawing nearer, it proved to be the top of the southwestern wall of
Musardu.   We fired our muskets, and entered the town.   We were
led up a street, or narrow lane, that brought us into the square in
which the mosque was situated.   Here were gathered the king Vomfeedolla, and the principal men of the town, to receive us.   My
Mandingo friends from Mahommadu opened the civilities of introduc-
tion with an elaborate speech; stating where I had come from, and
for what I had come; the power, learning and wealth of the Tibbabues   One of my friends, Barki, from Mahommadu, then engaged
to swear for me   that I had come for no ill purpose whatever, but
that I was moved entirely by an intelligent curiosity and friendly intercourse.   Dowilnyah's messengers then ,spoke in flattering terms
of my demeanor and liberality in their country, and the wishes of the
king, in consequence, that I should be treated in every way befitting
an illustrious stranger and his particular guest.   I had never before
been so complimented, and I became uneasy at the high importance
attached to the Tibbabue visit, fearing that great expectations in the
way of dashes or presents might be disappointed.   For my bundles,
bulky and pretentious in appearance, contained books, instruments
and clothes, more than the means upon which many hopes were then
founding and growing.   After the speeches were over, the king and
his people gave me repeated welcomes, with the peculiar privilege of
doing at Musardu whatever I was accustomed to do at Monrovia, a
large liberty, granted only to distinguished strangers.   An infinite
number of salaams and snapping of fingers then followed.   I was
soon disposed of, with luggage and carriers, in the king's court-yard,
with a house similar in structure and accommodation to the one at
Mahommadu.   We had learned the art of domiciling ourselves in

these towns, and in fifteen minutes everything wore the appearance of our having lived there for years. A number of Mandingo girls came to sing and dance for us, and we wasted some powder by way of returning the compliment.

As soon as night came on, we retired to rest; but our slumbers were disturbed by a harper, who in a tremulous minor key, improvised that since Musardu had been founded such a stranger had never visited it. The harp itself was a huge gourd, and a most unmusical "shell" it proved to be. It had three strings, the thrummings of which disquieted me on two accounts. First, the noise intrinsically disagreeable. Secondly, the expectations which that noise might be raising, as the bard in his *nocturne* declared my many gracious qualities, my courage, my wealth, and my liberality; upon the last two he dwelt with loud and repeated effort.

King Vomfeedolla in appearance has a mild, gentle countenance. His features would please those who are fond of a straight nose, broad forehead, thin lips, large and intelligent eyes, and an oval chin. Like all the Mandingoes, his skin is a smooth, gloosy black. In stature he is rather below the general towering height of his tribe. He does not possess the fiery energy of his royal Boozie brother, Dowilnyah, who, though many years his senior, far excels him in that respect.

In all councils Vomfeedolla seems to be entirely a listener, and to be directed and influenced by the older members of the royal family. He is said to be a great warrior; but the evidences around Musardu prove that if he is, he must belong to the unfortunate class of that profession.

The usual apparel or dress of the Mandingoes consists of four pieces —two pieces as a shirt and vest, and one large coat or toga worn over all; one pair of Turkish shaped trousers coming a little below the knees: sandals for the feet, which are sometimes beautifully worked; and a three-cornered cap for the head. These articles, made and worn as a Mandingo *only* can make and wear them, leave nothing to be desired, either as to taste and utility. This is said so far as the men are concerned But I must deplore a fashion observed by the women, in wrapping up their faces and bodies in a manner truly ungraceful and unhealthy, too.

Musardu is an exceedingly healthy place; there was not one prostrate, sickly person in the town There is, however, a disease which sometimes attacks individuals in a peculiar way; it is an affection of

the throat, causing a protuberance almost similar to what is called the
" king's evil. " I inquired the cause, and they imputed it to some·
thing that impregnates the water during the height of the dry season,
being the time when it mostly seizes persons.

The atmosphere of Musardu is very dry, and had a very favorable
effect upon my watches, which were declared at Monrovia, to be out
of order ; but as soon as I reached Musardu, every one of them began
to tick away in a clear and ringing manner.

Musardu, the capital of the Western Mandingoes, is in latitude
8° 27' 11" N., longitude 8° 24' 30" W. ; it is elevated two thousand
feet above the level of the sea and is situated amid gentle hills and
slopes. North and north-east two very high hills tower above the rest
several hundred feet. The population is between seven and eight
thousand, but the many villages and hamlets increase to a greater proportion. In the days of its prosperity, and before it had suffered from
the damaging effects of war, it had occupied a larger space, and was
not surrounded by any wall. Though it has lost its former importance,
Musardu is still considered as the capital of the Western Mandingoes,
and its name is never mentioned but in terms of patriotism and respect.
I often heard the old men of the town regret its past power and
wealth. They told me that what I then saw of Musardu was only the
ruins of a former prosperity. The town is laid off irregularly, with
very narrow and sometimes winding lanes or streets. These lanes or
streets cross each other in such a way as to give access to any part of
the town. The houses are built facing the lanes, and the rear space
is used as a yard for the horses and cattle. In the southwestern part
of the town is the mosque. The walls having been injured by the
weather, they had commenced to repair it. It is a quadrilateral building, surrounded by an oval-shaped wall, which is carried up eight
feet, and upon which rest the rafters of a large conical thatch-roof.
The interior space is thirty-two feet long and twenty two feet wide, and
nine feet high. It is laid off in four compartments, by three intermediate walls running the length of the building. These separate
spaces communicate with each other by three doors opening into each
intermediate wall. I do not know the purpose of the divisions, unless
it is to grade the faithful. It can scarcely accommodate more than one
hundred and twenty persons, and must therefore be devoted to the
most pious, or the leaders or teachers of Islam.

On Monday, the 14th of December, 1868, the King Vomfeedolla

held a military demonstration. He had summoned his infantry and cavalry from the nearest towns of Billelah, Yokkadu, Naalah, and Mahommadu. The exercises commenced about two o'clock P. M., in the large square of the town. The spectators and musicians had already assembled. All at once a trooper dashed past at full speed, as if he was reconnoitering the enemy. Several others followed, dispersing in different directions. The position of the enemy seeming to be determined, they soon returned. The trumpet then sounded, and a grand cavalry charge took place. Riding up in line, with musket in hand, they would deliver their fire, and canter off to the right and left, in order to allow the rear lines to do the same. As soon as the firing was over, they slung their muskets, and, rising in the saddle, drew their long knives in one hand and their crooked swords in the other; the horse, now urged to a headlong gallop by the voice, carries his rider, standing in the stirrups, with furious velocity into the heat of the battle. Their equipment is quite complete. They use saddles and bridles, and a peculiar and powerful bit; short stirrups; leather leggings, to which iron spurs are attached. The cavalry from all the towns, according to various reports, ought to amount to fifteen hundred.

In their open country, where the action of cavalry is greatly facil·itated by the long, gentle slopes, and wide, treeless plains, they would be no mean enemy. They often dismount, in order to act on foot. Each horse has a boy attendant to take care of him while his master is thus engaged In real action, I have been informed, the little boys of the defeated party often suffer the penalty of their participation. Yet these dangers do not deter the little fellows from going; for they are frequently able to ride off the field as soon as any symptoms of defeat are perceived.

The king seems to act for the most part with the infantry, for he rode in front and led them on. They came in deep array, and with great clamor, but without organization, being directed solely by a flag or ensign of blue cloth. I was sorry that I had no flag of ours to present them.

After their exercises were over, they requested us to fire our muskets; upon which we delivered regular volleys with bayonets fixed, both to their astonishment and delight, caused by the quickness with which we loaded our pieces, our certainty of fire—unlike their fusees, which were continually snapping—and the deeper report of our guns.

As soon as all the exercises were finished, the king then distributed the presents I had given him to the chiefs of the several military divisions.

Tuesday, the 15th of December, 1868. My Mandingo friends began to press me to trade with them. I informed them that I had nothing to trade with; that my gifts to the king and the principal men of the town had exhausted my means so closely as to scarcely leave me sufficient to enable me to return home. Nothing could convince them that I had not pieces of handkerchiefs and calicoes concealed in my bundles. They tried every method to induce me to trade; they carried me to their houses and would get out their small leathern bags; these bags contained from ten to fifteen large twisted gold rings, ("sannue"). They then offered me horses, and finally concluded by offering to sell me some pretty female slaves. I informed them that the Tibbabues did not keep slaves; that I had not come to trade, but merely to visit their country; that upon my return home I would persuade my people to come and trade with them. At the prospect of a number of Tibbabues coming to their country to trade, they were exceedingly satisfied.

From trade we passed to war and politics, and having satisfied all their inquiries in these two particular points with respect to the Tibbabues, they made me acquainted with some of their wars and feuds. They had a special cause of grievance against a certain Mandingo chief whose name was Ibrahima, or Blamer Sissa, and who lived north-east, and three days' walk from Musardu, at a large town called Madina.

It appears that Blamer Sissa came from Madina to visit his uncle, Amalah, who was then residing at Musardu, and that he was treated with great civility and distinction by the Musardu people; that being a powerful young prince, they solicited his aid against some Kaffres, or unbelievers, living over the eastern hills; that in compliance with their solicitation he went back to Madina, and soon returned to Musardu, bringing with him his cavalry and infantry, a numerous and formidable mass, who, in the end, came nigh doing their friends at Musardu as much evil as they had done the Kaffres, whom they had mutually agreed to plunder.

Blamer Sissa stripped Musardu of every thing valuable, and even carried off nearly all the pretty young women of that town.

On Thursday, the 16th of December, 1868, at seven o'clock P.M.,

Chancellor came running to my house to inform me that several suspicious persons, with their horses or jackasses, were lurking about the
north-western side of the town ; that they had sought admittance, but
it had been refused them ; that they had reported themselves traders,
but the town people were on the alert, believing them to be Blamer
Sissa's spies, who were only skulking around in order to gain all the
intelligence they could, and carry it to their friends, who were supposed to be in strong force behind the north-eastern hills. Next
morning, Friday, the 17th of December, the strange people were
indeed seen on a hill north-west of the town, and cold must have
been the sleep they had of it the previous night for the thermometer
stood at 52° at four A.M A council was held how to act. Some proposed to send the young men out to kill them. Afterward it was more
wisely determined to go out and order them to take their traffic and
depart with it at once.

We accordingly went out, and after the usual salutations, they were
given plainly to understand that neither they nor their trade could
enter Musardu, and that they must depart without delay. But our
strange merchants were not to be frightened off in that manner. They
insisted that they had come for no evil purpose whatever, but simply
to prosecute their trade. The conferences were prolonged until mid-
day. While the conversation was going on, I had an opportunity to
survey the suspicious group of new-comers. It consisted of two sturdy
little jackasses, with enormous packs, containing what looked like, and
afterwards proved to be French blue baft, and five men. The one
who acted as guide and interpreter was one of Blamer Sissa's people,
and he alone served to confirm our suspicions. The other four were
tall, black, good-featured people. One of them had his face and head
bound up with a piece of white cotton, after the peculiar manner of
some of the Arabs of the desert. They were all Mohammedans. I
learned that they had come from the Senegal, had been to Futtah,
passed through Kanghkah, and had obtained this guide from Madina,
to show them to Musardu. I began to be interested in them. The
Musardu people, however, remained deaf to every argument, and the
Senegal merchants were compelled to pack their bundles on their
asses, and go. Nay, the town people, to assure themselves of their
going, followed them some distance. But the sight of such large
bundles in such a time of need and self-interest, had sown the seeds
of discord ; and there was much contention now among the Musardu

people themselves.   Some were for allowing the merchants to enter
the town.   Others opposed it, alleging that such were always the artifices of Blamer Sissa when he wished to take a strong town ; that he
always sent some of his people ahead, who, under pretext of wishing
to trade, introduced themselves into the town in order to open the
gates at night to his forces.   The contention grew so warm that they
even came to blows.

On Saturday, the 19th of December, about nine o'clock A. M., news
came to the town that the merchants had returned. We went out and
found it really so ; and when the order was repeated to them to go
away, they absolutely refused, declaring that they had come to trade ;
that having left neither mother nor wife behind, the Musardu people
might kill them if they wished to do so. Their firmness overcame the
first determination of the Musardu people, who, after nearly having
another quarrel among themselves, gave the merchants leave to trade
outside of the town—a permission with which our Senegal friends
seemed to be quite satisfied.   It was difficult at the first to make out
who our merchants were.   No one could understand their language
except the Mandingo interpreter from Madina, and it was this man
who caused them to be seriously suspected, for he was one of Blamer
Sissa's soldiers.   These poor merchants, therefore, might have been
subserving Blamer Sissa's purposes, without the least knowledge of it
themselves.   It was solely their interpreter that marked them as suspected persons.

On Monday, the 21st of December, our Musardu friends, after all
their blustering determination against the merchants, admitted them
into the town.   Interest and avarice overcame all their patriotism and
caution. The two jackass loads of goods, not unlike the Trojan horse,
were dragged into the town, and if Blamer Sissa had any designs on
Musardu, they were accomplished.

Both in policy and energy Blamer Sissa seemed superior to the
Musardu people ; for in addition to the trouble he had already given
them, and even the recent threats he had made, he knew how to
introduce his own people in the town, who could give any intelligence
with respect to Musardu he might desire.   He is not the first prince
who has taken a city by means of a jackass-load of merchandise.   The
Musardu people sent a thundering message of defiance and insult to
Blamer Sissa, making the largest use of me to break it up. They sent
him word that they were not at all dependent on him for trade or any

thing else; that the Tibbabues were about to open trade with them, and would be their friends in peace and war; that even then a Tibbabue was negotiating that particular business in Musardu. They then took pains to exhibit the arms and means with which the destruction of Madina might sooner or later be accomplished. My muskets with their bayonets, my revolvers, and my person, were severally shown as designed for that especial object.

I was purposely questioned aloud as to the military resources of the Tibbabues : the little guns that fired any number of times without loading, and the big guns that burnt up cities at the distance of miles. I gave such answers as I hope will make Blamer Sissa less troublesome to Musardu for the future.

It might be thought impolitic that I did not refrain from expressing myself as being in either party's favor. In this part of Africa, if hostilities are lukewarm, neutrality is possible ; but where it burns with the flame of recent and bitter injuries, you are absorbed by either one side or the other, or torn to pieces by both.

The Musardu people are unfortunately situated. On the north they expect war with Blamer Sissa, and on the east hostilities have never ceased ; the west and south-west are still open to them. It is the latter direction that opens itself to our enterprise, and promises much to our commercial prosperity. The chief articles of trade are gold, bullocks, hides, horses and country cloths of every variety of dye and texture. Gold is worn extravagantly by the Mandingo ladies of Musardu. The earrings are so large and weighty as to require a narrow piece of leather to brace them up to their head-bands, so that the part of the ring in the ear may not make an unseemly hole, as sometimes happen when this necessary support is neglected. Gold is certainly abundant, and would form a lucrative trade between Musardu and Liberia. I gave twelve sheets of writing-paper (katahsee, and four yards of calico for a large gold twist ring   Had I came purposely to trade and had gone through the usual practice of "jewing down," I could have purchased it for less. These rings are perfectly pure, the natives never mixing any kind of alloy in the manufacturing of them. Many of my friends wondered at my making presents of watches, music-boxes, and calicoes when the articles might have been exchanged for gold or slaves ; but as I was determined that the money should be religiously appropriated to the purpose for which it was sent out, I steadily refused every proffer excepting such few things as I could conveniently bring back as samples of the production and industry of the country.

To carry on trade safely, free from the risks and interruptions incident to a country peopled by barbarians and semi-barbarians, and divided into so many jarring interests, it would be necessary to establish four trading forts—two in the Boozie and Barline countries, which would purchase country cloths, raw cotton, camwood, rice, palm oil, etc. ; and two in the Mandingo country, where gold, bullocks, country cloths, and horses could be purchased at such rates as would amply remunerate for all the trouble. expense, and consumption of time necessary in such traffic.   The individuals living in the forts would be abundantly supplied with food, as rice is produced in surplus quantities in the Boozie and Barline countries.   Even the expense of clothing would be trifling, if they would use the cloth of the country.   The natives declare that they would be glad to have such establishments among them.   These forts would also second and strengthen any missionary effort that might be made out there; indeed, the two establishments could be made to work admirably together.   The support, protection, and moral and material influence which would be exerted in the respective operations of each, would insure permanence and success.   We would do well to commence the use of jackasses; indeed, it would be indispensable for the portage or transportation of luggage.   The Senegal traders at Musardu carried very large packs of blue cotton on their two sturdy little animals. Horses and bullocks would form no unimportant part of the trade. Mahommadu is a regular beef market.

The auriferous or gold district of this part of Manding is said to be principally at Buley.   Upon my first inquiry, I was told that Buley was a week's journey eastward; but upon my continuing to prosecute my inquiries respecting that country, Buley was immediately removed one week's walk further, making it two weeks' walk; and through hostile and dangerous districts, the people of which, as my Musardu friends informed me, would exact toll from me for passing through their country.   Every difficulty was conjured up that was conceived to be sufficient to extinguish all interest for further inquiry, or to intimidate my going in that direction.

However, my Mandingo cousins have no doubt misrepresented the whole matter; for gold not only exists at Buley, but right there in their own country—otherwise I do not think it could be so plentiful

among themselves, since they have little or no communication with
the east.

At Buley, it is found mixed in fine grains with the superficial de-
posit. No one is allowed to sweep or pick up anything in another's
yard. The gold is separated by fanning and washing; it is then
smelted and twisted, and ready for sale or use. They show some
skill and taste in the preparation of these rings, and they are really
worth their weight in gold. Our friends are sometimes equally skill-
ful in preparing counterfeits, as my nitric acid had several occasions
to prove. Impositions of this kind are generally punished by heavy
fines.

In going to Buley, you pass successively Bendalah—where a very
fine species of country cloth is made, of striped figure, and usually
worn by the women—Tangalah, Tutah, and Gehway. Now, if these
towns are situated from each other at the usual distance of Africans
—namely, a day's walk—Buley is but four days' walk east from Musardu, which I take to be the fact, despite the industry of my friends to
prove to the contrary. Unlike Musardu, it is a wooded country.
This fact may give us some idea of the extent of those treeless hills
and plains eastward. They are said to extend further north than in
any other direction, where, indeed, cow-dung is used for fuel. The
population of Buley is Mandingo. Gold is also obtained north of
Blamer Sissa's town, at Wasalah.

My friends now tried again to provoke me to trade, offering the
same articles they had offered before—gold, horses, and female
slaves. Indeed, this is all the Mandingoes of Musardu had to offer
by way of trade. Not a bullock or a country cloth was to be seen,
though these things are notoriously the articles of merchandise belonging to Musardu. Everything liable to be seized in war from its being
too bulky to be quickly removed or concealed, sad experience has
taught them to keep out of reach, in some friendly Boozie town in
the rear of the Vukkah hills; while nothing but the war-horse, and
articles easy to be hid or carried off, are kept at Musardu. At every
house can be seen muskets, cutlasses, powder horns, war-belts, and
war-coats, a powerful large bow, and four or five large quivers filled
with poisoned arrows. I have seen them prepare the poison with
which the points of the arrows are smeared over. It is a vegetable
poison, consisting of one bulbous root twice as large as an onion, and
two different kinds of small vines, It is boiled in a pot to a thick or

gummy consistence, the color of which is black.   It is said to be so
fatal that if it wounds so much as the tip ends of the fingers it is certain death.   The preparers of this fearful means of savage warfare
but too clearly explained to me its effects before death completely
ensues: the bleeding at the nose and ears; its nauseous attack on the
stomach, and consequent spitting; the final despair of the individual
in lying down, with his eyes set in a vacant death-stare—all of which
was imitated with a terrible fidelity to the truth, and as one of the
most horrible means of barbarous warfare.

This part of Mandingo is the country of the horse.   There are
two sizes: the large horse, used for show and parade, and the small
horse, used for war.   The latter is a hardy, strong little animal,
capable, in his country, of bearing great fatigue.   In battle, I am informed, he kicks and bites in a furious manner, and that when his
master makes a capture of a fine young lady, he willingly receives
the additional burden, and gallops off faster than ever.   These
horses are certainly well treated and cared for; and if Musardu is not
characteristic for cleanliness, it is because the horse and his master
equally occupy and almost equally litter up that capital.

I tried my best to obtain some data by which an approximate notion
might be formed of the age of the city ; but in matters of chronology
our friends have been sadly careless.   None of them could give the
least intelligent hint. · They said that the grandfather of the oldest
man in the town declared that the town was there when he was born,
and that all the other towns sprang from this one.   Its antiquity is an
undoubted matter among themselves. I was shown their large market-
place outside of the town, a few hundred yards from the south-western
gate. From the space it occupied, it would easily have contained eight
or ten thousand people.   The respective places where each commodity was exhibited for sale was pointed out : country cloths, cattle,
gold, (dust and manufactured), slaves, grain, salt, of which there were
two kinds—the slab or rock-salt, which came on camels from the
north-east, and our fine salt, gotten from the coast ; ostrich feathers ;
leather, in the beautiful and soft tanning of which the Mandingoes
are particularly expert ; ivory, cotton, tobacco, and an infinite variety
of domestic articles were all named, and the different places where
they were sold designated.

But war has abolished every sign of this commercial activity and
life, and has introduced in its stead a barren space filled with weeds,

grass, and the broken skulls and skeletons of enemies—a desperate battle having been fought there between the Musardu people, aided by Blamer Sissa, and the eastern Mandingoes.

The soil of the hills of Musardu is composed of reddish clay and sand, with boulders of iron ore intermixed. On the north-eastern side of the town are some large masses of .bl ck and gray granite. The plains are a whitish clay, and the very soil for a plow, being free from almost every obstruction. The light tillage of the natives never goes more than four or five inches, with their little short-handled hoes.

About February or March, and sometimes sooner, the high grass and wild cane are cut down, to rot and manure the soil. Near the planting season, these vegetable fertilizers are turned in with the hoe; and from the crops of rice, of which there are three kinds, potatoes, ground-nuts, onions, peas and beans, large gourds, corn, pumpkins, etc., it must answer abundantly the purposes of agriculture. Tobacco is grown in plots, wherever a stream of water offers itself for frequent irrigation. The rubbish and ashes of the town form excellent beds for this plant. They are generally laid out with great care, and watered three times a day. The Mandingoes are the great tobacco raisers and snuff-makers of the country. They supply both themselves and the Boozies.

Musardu is singularly free from grasshoppers, rats, and mice, owing to the number of hawks that crowd the limbs of a solitary tree that may be standing here and there. Want of trees compels them to perch themselves on rocks, and when these are all occupied, they may be seen to cover the ground in dark patches. There are also large birds that particularly belong to the grassy plains of Musardu. They go in flocks of eight or twelve. In size, they are as large as American geese, and, on account of their weight, do not fly very high, nor do they make long passages at a time. When they alight on the ground, they are enabled, by the length of their necks, to discover you before you can get within gunshot of them. Their hearing, however, is not very acute; for we have often crept up the brow of the hill, and come upon them suddenly. They are a very sagacious and shy bird; and though I and my Congoes tried our marksmanship many times, we were entirely unable to procure one of them. The Mandingoes are scarcely ever able to kill them. Their color is white, with a black band across their back and wings; and when flying, their leader never ceases to make a cawing noise. They are very gawky in their movements when walking on the ground, caused by their long necks, giving their heads a deliberative nod with every step they take.

The Mandingoes are very attentive to their farming interests They are, however, more given to trade than to manual labor. The leading vice of a Mandingo is avarice, which, by however much it is stimulated, the present state of the country affords him but little means to gratify. Nothing can be accumulated among themselves that war does not instantly dissipate.   Nevertheless, they are quick and intelligent, easy to be managed by persuasion, and they offer to Liberia a more speedy prospect of assimilation and union than any other tribe with which I am acquainted.   A strong moral advantage is already gained, from their being a reading and writing people, practicing a communication of ideas and an interchange of thought by means of the Arabic.   They have a natural reverence for learning and mental superiority, and they never fail to respect it, whether it accords with their belief or not.   No rudeness, no indecent and wrangling intolerance. was ever shown me during my stay among them.   No difference of religion ever made them diminish the respect, attention, and hospitality which they conceived were due me.   One of my Congo carriers is of the Baptist persuasion, and he used to make himself heard every morning, even to my own annoyance, by loud orisons. Still, our Mohammedan Mandingoes said nothing.   It was respected as a prayer, and it was known to be a Christian prayer.

On the 19th of December, I visited Billelah Kaifal, Kandah's native town.   In size it is nearly as large as Musardu.   The houses are in a better condition ; but in all other respects it resembles the parent city—the narrow lanes, horse stables, gardens, etc. The town seemed densely populated, even with children

The next day we started from Billelah for our home, Musardu, visiting on our way another town, Yockkadu.   This town is about a quarter of the size of Musardu, and similar in its arrangements, customs, and habits.   The chief of this town, Vawfulla, proved to be very hospitable.

On Sunday, the 21st of December, my Boozie attendants grew impatient to return home, and even prepared to leave me.   I gave them full liberty to go if they wished, since I did not intend to make the least move until I had finished my business.   The sky had been so hazy as to prevent my taking any observations.   The fine dust of the Harmattans, together with the vast volumes of smoke and cinders from the grassy hills and plains that were burning, rendered it a difficult matter to take observations. This was the cause of my delaying to return, and the consequent dissatisfaction of my Boozies, a people who were not willing to be kept from their homes any length of time. Chancellor, however, was enabled to appease their impatience by three yards of calico.

Having now exhausted the time, as well as almost all the means which had been assigned to carry out this expedition, I began to think of returning home; yet I must confess there was nothing more contrary to my wishes. Had it not been that family responsibilities demanded my return home, I should have still, with or without means, prosecuted my journey eastward — a direc ion which I have always had the presentiment contains the prosperity and welfare of Liberia.

On Friday, the 25th of December, at eight A. M., we bade farewell to Musardu, and arrived at Mahommadu at six P. M. Here we passed several days, in order to take observations and to see the market. This market is held every Wednesday, outside of the eastern wall.

On Wednesday, the 30th, this market took place. It contained three hundred head of cattle, which were offered at three or four dollars a head in our money. The usual articles of rice, onions, palmoil, cotton, country cloth, tobacco, and iron were present. There were a number of slaves for sale, especially children. A pretty little Mandingo girl, about nine years of age, was sent to my house with one of my boys, in order that I might purchase her. She cost 9000 kolu, or about $15 in our money. I was curious to know how she became a slave, as Mandingoes are seldom ever enslaved. I declined to buy her, on the ground that Tibbabues never held slaves. The child herself seemed to be disappointed; for she showed that she preferred falling into my hands in preference to her own people. The Mandingoes are harsher to their slaves than the Boozies. Among the Boozies it is difficult to distinguish the slave by any mark of dress or usage; but the Mandingoes, though not excessively cruel, have drawn the lines of difference in so strong a manner th t you can not fail to perceive them.

A great many cattle remained unsold. The season of the dries is very severe on them, and they sometimes die from overdriving. Several died the next day after the market was over. They are the large, reddish, long-horned cattle, which we usually buy from the interior. The highlands, from which they come, explains why they do not thrive so well as the black, short-horned, and sturdy cattle of the coast, known among us as the "leeward cattle."

It was at this town that I first experienced the hospitality of these people in their own country. Our Mandingoes are Mohammedans ; but they have an invincible partiality for Tibbabues, who are known to be Christians, and the people of the book. It is also well known that there is some difference in the creeds or beliefs; yet the unbelieving Tibbabue is sure to be housed, fed and befriended in a manner that is not always practised among the faithful themselves.

While they were repairing the wall of Mahommadu I was requested to carry some of the mortar and place it in the wall, that it might be said that "a Tibbabue helped to build these walls." I contributed all I could to make them impregnable.

During our stay there, we were also taken to their foundry, where they were busily engaged in preparing iron for the market. The pieces of pure iron taken from the furnace are again heated; they are then reduced to a long triangular shape by pounding them with large heavy stones—a process simple and laborious enough and a work which is entirely left to slaves.

Blacksmithing. such as the making of stirrups, bits, spurs, etc., is done by the Mandingoes themselves, as being a mechanical art too noble to be performed by slaves.

On Thursday, the 31st of December, we left Mahommadu, and reached Vukkah at half-past four o'clock P M. We were now among the Boozies again. The Vukkah hills run N. E. and S. W. The towns of Mahommadu and Vukkah stand at the very foot of the south-eastern slope. I am informed that many other Mandingo and Boozie towns are situated on the same side of this range. At Mahommadu, the plain, in a south-east direction, is only interrupted by swells and rolling hills, rising and running in every direction, and marked by no particular feature, except the reddish color of the soil, and their summits ridged with the dwarfish prairie tree before mentioned The plains are white clay, mixed with bed of iron ore. At Mahommadu, the south-east slope strikes the plain at a great angle ; but at Vukkah, it rests upon a series of small table-lands that extend out a half mile before they finally come down into the plains. The vast spaces of grass and reddish soil are relieved by patches of dense vegetation marking the gullies and ravines. Heavy blocks of granite are set in the sides of the Vukkah hills, awaiting only to be loosened by the rains to roll from their places to the bottom. At night, the whole country seems on fire, from the burning of the grass.

On January 1st, 1869, we left Vukkah, and reached Ballatah at two P. M. On the road, we passed several streams of water, flowing over granite beds, with a temperature of 58° to 60°, Fahrenheit. We had also passed over three plains, rising one above another, in which lines of trees traced off curious plots and divisions, as if they were purposely laid out for farming. The spaces were filled in with green grass and scattering clumps of trees.

January 2d. From Ballatah, we traveled to the village of Gazzahbue.

January 3d, 1869. From Gazzahbue, we reached Gubbewallah, Dowilnyah's residence. The king was still at Ziggah Porrah Zue; but in three days he returned to his own town. Here, though anxious to hasten home, I was obliged to spend some time; since it is contrary to politeness to hurry away from the town of a great chief without having resided with him two or three weeks. All my friends who had arrived from Ziggah Porrah Zue were delighted to see me, and they began to grow solicitous about my returning to their country again. Promises of all kinds were made if I would return; promises of a very peculiar kind were made by the king if I would only return.

The ladies of Wymar seemed no less anxious respecting me; and they frequently asked me why, since I possessed he means of making so many presents, I did not have a number of women to sing and clap hands and proclaim my importance after the fashion of their great men. To which I replied that such was not the custom of '' Weegees,'' or Americans. They were, however, unwilling that I should go through their country ' unhonored and unsung;'' they therefore proposed to compliment me with this custom, and merrily fell to clapping and singing; then raising their right hands to the sky rent the air with their acclamations of praise and flattery.

On Monday, the 25th of January, we took leave of King Dowilnyah. The king presented us with several large country cloths, and a very large and heavy ivory. He had also sent for a horse; but we declined receiving the presents, as we had no one to carry them. He would have furnished us carriers, had it not been that they would have to pass through the Domars, with whom they were not on friendly terms.

About four o'clock P M., we reached Boe. Here we spent a day to rest. On Wednesday, the 27th January, at four o'clock P.M , we came to Nubbewah's town.   King Nubbewah was not at home when we arrived; but late in the afternoon this sick and feeble old man came stalking into the town, followed by his head warrior and a number of young men all armed.

In the evening they held a council, and Nubbewah himself delivered a speech with a violence of gesture and voice that little corresponded with the languid, sickly frame from which it came. Mischief was brewing; but where or on whom it would first light, no one of our party could conjecture. We only hoped that it would keep to its first purpose, and not fall on us

It was a very clear moonlight.   About twelve o'clock, Chancellor, who was generally very vigilant whenever there happened to be an unusual stir among the natives, detected one of the young men with his cutlass gleaming in the moonlight, stealthily lifting up our doormat. He was suddenly questioned as to what he wanted, which threw him into such confusion that he was only able to stammer out something about fire, and quickly withdrew   Several persons were then seen passing and repassing in the king's court-yard.   We immediately concluded that such movements boded no good to us.   We aroused our party and prepared for a general onslaught, which we every moment expected; such being the usual method of these people's attacks. Nubbewah's town contains three thousand people, men, women, and children. The houses are crowded together. The king's own department is shut off from the rest of the town by high fences, and strongly guarded with a number of large Mandingo dogs. It is every way so situated that a petty wickedness can be committed covertly and conveniently enough, and nobody be the wiser.

All the houses are bamboo, and would burn like tinder. I therefore instructed my people that, should Nubbewah attack us, we must immediately set fire to the house we were in, and discharge our muskets into those who came at us first ; that amid the hubbub of fire, smoke, and fighting, our chances for escape would be as good as any one s else ; that we must make for the gate nearest to our house, and march all night for Bokkasah.   Our knapsacks were strapped on, our muskets in hand and the torches blazing in the fire   There was more passing and repassing and distinct whisperings. Success with these people depends upon surprise ; our bustling preparation placed a surprise entirely out of the question.   In fifteen minutes all was quiet.   Every one instinctively felt that the dangerous moment had passed ; yet we kept on our guard.

The next morning we went to the king, who put on a most intelligent innocence. We made him a small present and immediately left his town. We arrived at Bokkasah at four o'clock P. M.

So far as the matter of carrying arms is concerned, it is always better to observe the usage of the natives. Arms always form a part of the dress of barbarians. The more formidable you can make yourself appear, the better for your peace and safety on these highways of African travel. To seem harmless does not always invoke forbearance; it sometimes suggests plots and attempts on life and property. It was that too much reliance on the simple-heartedness and good feelings of untutored barbarians that got Seymore's right hand nearly slashed off. It is preferable to try every way to induce sheir good-will, and at the same time to appear to be ready to resist their ill-will. Every person I met on the road was girded with a heavy iron sword, a quiver thrown over the shoulders full of poisoned arrows, and a powerful bow. Adopting this example, I became a moving arsenal. I walked through the whole Boozie country with my bayonet fixed to my musket, my revolvers belted so as to be seen and feared at the same time, my sword swinging and clanging at my side ; and when, to prove my *prestige* in arms, I was asked to fire my revolvers, I would draw and blaze away, several barrels going off almost at the same time—a serious defect to be sure, but regarded in a very different light by my friends. The bulging fullness of my country coat was attributed to the concealment of similar arms, ready to go off at all points. This swaggering style was not without effect ; for it was said that I had money to give my friends and arms to fight my enemies. I had almost forgotten to mention that I was informed by Dowilnyah that five principal chiefs were concerned in the assault on Seymore ; that not one of them was now living ; that their death was accounted as the punishment of God for this act of wickedness.

Seymore, relaxing all caution on account of the uniform good treatment he had received from the natives, thought them incapable of a different conduct. He was seriously convinced to the contrary. When villainy of this kind is to be perpetrated, the greatest secrecy among those who are privy to it is preserved. It is always the act of a few ; for the feelings of the mass seem to be averse to such doings. Seymore's affair was mentioned in terms of reprobation by all who conversed with me in the matter. Comma's own son strenuously denied to me that his father had any part in the matter ; though it is a fact notorious throughout the country that his father was a principal actor, and that the whole plot was concocted at the town of Boe.

From Bokkasah we came to Fissahbue, on Monday the 8th of February, 1869 On Tuesday, the 9th we arrived at Zolu. King Momoru had not, up to this time, been able to effect a reconciliation between the parties. Every day they made reprisals on each other. While I was there, the Boozies succeeded in capturing several persons belonging to the Barline people. The wars of these people are however, not attended with any sanguinary results. They consist mostly in surprising a few individuals where they can be suddenly come upon. Sometimes the roads are waylaid wherever their respective traders are supposed to pass. These, together with some other petty annoyances, constitute their principal mode of warfare. The large walled towns are seldom taken. Pitched battles are seldom fought; and even when these people may be said to take the open field, most is done by some war chief by way of displaying his individual prowess. If they were to indulge too much in war, they could never have the numerous and large markets with which their country is everywhere dotted.

Tuesday, the 16th of February, 1869, we started from Zolu, passed through the Boozie towns of Yahwuzue, Kaulitodah, Wuzugahzeah. On the road we met Beah, our Mandingo guide, with some Bokkasah traders, who informed that the Americans had carried war against Mana. We halted at Powlazue. Wednesday, the 17th of February, we passed Zolaghee and its large creek, running over a bed of red feldspar granite. Thousands of fish, known among us as ''bonies,'' were swimming close to shore, not at all annoyed by the people who were bathing in the same water.

We halted at Moffotah. Thursday, the 18th of February, we passed Malang, Ballah, and Dahtazue, and halted at a small village. On Friday, the 19th of February, we reached Barkomah. Saturday, the 20th, leaving Barkomah, we passed through several villages and the town of Nessahbeah. We halted at Sellayo, at six o clock P. M.

Sunday, the 21st, starting from Sellayo, we passed Barpellum, where we saw a man who had been wounded in four places with a cutlass. He had been beset in the road by unknown persons ; showing after all, the danger and insecurity of the roads, as well as the folly of traveling unarmed. At four P. M., we reached Totoquella, the residence of King Momoru, where we were received with every demonstration of joy and hospitality. Here we spent some time, in order to avail ourselves of the opportunity of completing calculations of longitude, which, when we were at Boporu, we had been unable to do on account of the weather.

While we were staying at Totoquella, some of the king's people killed an elephant; and instead of beef we had elephant for dinner. The part regarded as a delicacy, and upon which we dined heartily, was the proboscis. He had not yielded his life in a tame, unbecoming manner; his death was attended with the flight of his enemies, the smashing up of gun-stocks, the stamping and rending af saplings. One musket had its barrel literally bent to an angle of ninety degrees. The narrow escape of the hunters themselves suggested to me what might have happened, had I attacked the herd of elephants feeding in the cotton-fields of Ballatah. There the country is open and exposed; here the friendly woods and jungle offer the hunter immediate concealment and protection. The elephants upon the highlands pertinaciously go in herds, and scarcely ever allow themselves to be separated. Intrepid elephant-hunters, accustomed to display firmness and certainty within six paces of a furious charge, are invited to try their prowess with the Ballatah elephants.

Sierra Leone.

Though what follows is not concerning Liberia, the contiguity of Sierra Leone renders it of interest, and I therefore present you persons of note in Sierra Leone, a British colony, north of Liberia: Rev. F. G. Snelson, A.M., Ph.D., and Presiding Elder in the A. M. E. Church; Rev. George Dove Decker, one of the leading pastors of Freetown, in the A. M. E. Church, and other ministers, with a few laymen of wealth and education. Were it our purpose to go outside of Liberia, much material could be gathered from this colony. The Africans in this district are intellectual and wealthy. The Timnee, Mandingoes and Fullahs predominate.

MINISTERS AND REPRESENTATIVES.

Presentation.

———

This volume is presented to honor and assist the Right Reverend Henry McNeal Turner, Doctor of Divinity and Doctor of Canonical Laws, Bishop of Africa for the African M. E. Church, champion of Liberia and defender of the Negro race—together with many young men, who are laboring in Liberia to give the little Republic prominence as a nation. We name Messrs. Dunbar, King, the Potters, Houstons, Gibsons, Diggs, Johnsons, Dennises, Paynes, and others, working to dispel darkness, remove prejudice, and defend truth—as touching this Negro Republic.

Yours for the uplifting of the race,

WILLIAM H. HEARD,

Author.

ADDENDA.

EXPORTS AND IMPORTS.

The exports of Liberia are $1,200,000 per annum. The exports are mostly raw materials, such as rubber, palm oil, palm kernels, pyasava, kola nuts, coffee, ginger, hides, cocoa, etc., etc.

Imports which are greater than the exports are bread-stuff, building materials, dry goods, etc., etc.

On page 11, line 9, the word "Fourali" should be "Fourah."

On page 48, line 11, the word "Conference" should be "Legislature."

On page 71, line 33, the word "Haineses" should be "Harrises."

LIST OF ILLUSTRATIONS.

CONTENTS.